MY SOUTHAMPTON

Cover: Hop Picking at Binstead, Hampshire about 1922. My aunt Angelina who was Italian.

My
Southampton
in the Twenties & Thirties

Jim Bellows

ELSP

Published in 2001 by
ELSP
1 The Shambles
Bradford on Avon
Wiltshire

Design and typesetting by
Ex Libris Press

Printed by Cromwell Press
Trowbridge

ISBN 1 903341 67 1

Contents

PREFACE

This book contains my memories of the nineteen-twenties and nineteen-thirties in Southampton. Those were the so-called good old days, but they were hard times. However, compared to my mother's childhood, mine was a piece of cake. To illustrate this, I have prefaced the book with a story of my mother's life as narrated to one of her grandchildren, Sara King.

Jim Bellows
Southampton
March 2001

1

MY GRANNY

My Granny was born in 1894 and her parents lived in a tied cottage in very poor conditions. In 1909, when she was 15, her baby brother was born. The wise lady at the end of the road delivered him. When the baby was two days old her mother became ill and Granny had to send for the doctor. She wore no shoes and a long skirt down to her ankles. She ran across the fields to fetch the doctor. When she returned home she found that the house was collapsing and she and the Doctor carried her mother and the baby out of the house and put them into a disused pigsty in the garden. Here her mother died and the children continued to live until they were re-housed.

My Granny was the eldest in the family and so she had to look after everyone after her mother was buried. The coffin was taken to the church by horse and cart. That night her father left the children alone in the house and they were all very frightened and decided to go and look for him. My Gran strapped the baby to her back and set off along the dusty road. As they walked, a bread van, drawn by a horse, passed them; as it continued along the bumpy road a loaf of bread fell out of the back of the van. The hungry children quickly picked it up and took it home.

She continued to look after the children for the next two years. Her father had taken to drink and did not give her enough money to feed the children so they had to beg for food. When they begged at the convent they were given a piece of bread and cheese each.

Granny had to plough fields by hand and pick watercress to earn money. When picking watercress she waded waist deep into the water, her long skirt floating on the top. Sitting in the riverbank she put it into bunches and, still very wet, she walked to the market in Wareham to sell it.

When she was 17 she was married. Her husband, my Grandfather, came from Southampton. They travelled from Dorset to Southampton by horse and cart, which took two days. At night they slept under the cart. It was pea-picking time and they spent their honeymoon with all the other pea pickers at Botley, in a long hut divided into cubicles by sacks.

After this, they lived in Southampton in a terraced house in Bargate Street, which was part of the old Southampton Wall. Their house had no garden, the front door opened onto the path. On washing day all the mums in the area put wet washing in their prams and had to take it down to the park opposite Debenham's where washing lines were hung between the trees.

Granny could not read or write but Gramps taught her using the Bible.

During the war they were bombed out of their house and moved to Hedge End. Her older boys and husband were costermongers.

She died at the age of 72 after bringing up seven children, five boys and two girls.

2

HOME LIFE

I was born in 1917 in a terraced house in a little court called Tower Place, near the Bargate. My family consisted of my father, Tom, who was a 'Coster' – a fruit and vegetable seller. He was a smart, good-looking man and wore clothes typical of the period: narrow-bottomed trousers with a flap across the front which used to do up with a button each side. The same style was worn in the Navy, only with bell-bottom trousers. He also wore a sleeved waistcoat, similar to those worn by railway porters, only more stylish. He always wore a silk paisley neckerchief, but he would never wear a tie. He said that was like wearing a 'collar and hames' – that is a horse collar with brass stems going around it. He also wore a cap, and I think he quite fancied himself.

My mother came from Romany stock. She was dark and handsome with long black hair. She wore black lace-up boots, which reached almost to her knees. She had an eighteen-inch waist. I know this because mum was proud of her figure and wore tight lace-up corsets to show it off. My Grandmother used to say, "If you pull 'em any tighter you'll cut yourself in half!" My mother was a flower seller and used to stand on the pavement at The Junction. She also used to 'walk' (a word used when selling from door to door) around the richer areas of the town.

I had an older brother Tom, a younger sister Lily Louisa,

named after mum, and Walter or 'Wally' was the youngest. Two more brothers, Bill and Len, and another sister Maureen, joined the family later.

My paternal grandmother also lived with us. She was half-Romany, her mother being Romany and her father a town dweller. Her parents both died young and she was brought up by her grandparents.

This is my grandmother with her feathered hat, gold earrings and five-shilling piece made into a broach. She was well known around Southampton and the Echo *paid her a tribute on her death.*

My earliest memories are of Tom and myself. Those of Lou and Walt came later.

There were just thirteen houses in Tower Place, ten on one side and three on the other. The reason for this was, at the top end, there was an old derelict factory. I never knew what it used to manufacture, but over the years it made a good rubbish dump! Strangely enough, as children, we rarely climbed the walls to play inside it.

Each house had a small garden, or at least a yard, about sixteen feet long and seven feet wide, which was covered in concrete. At the end of the garden, or yard, was an eight-feet-high wall, which extended the whole length of the court on both sides. This left a court between the walls about nine feet wide. It was paved with concrete slabs either side of a central concrete gully. Every Monday the council workman arrived pushing a hand truck containing a water hydrant, brooms, shovels and a hose. After connecting the hydrant and turning the water on with a big iron key, he scrubbed and washed down the courtyard. Of course, when we children were on holiday we had great fun running up a down the gully. We would sometimes make paper boats and run to the bottom of the courtyard to stop them going down the drain.

I spent the first twelve years of my life in our court. There was only one entrance to our house, which was a gate let into the wall. Once in, you were in a world of your own, surrounded by brick walls. On the left, as you went in, was the toilet. The pan was encased with wood with wood across the top and a hole cut over the pan. The top was handy because there was no light, window or ventilation, so, when it was dark, you could take a bit of candle with you, pour some of the candle grease on the top and stick the candle to it. This served two purposes, one was light, the other was to warm your hands when it was cold.

Another amenity was a four-inch nail driven into the wall on which the toilet paper was speared. The paper squares were either bits of the *Echo* or, *The News of The World*. There wasn't a lot of waste in those days!

Next to the toilet was what we called the wash-house. Inside it was a brick-built copper. The copper itself was a big, cast-iron bowl set into the brickwork. A grill was fixed under the copper for fire. Everything was burned here except coal or coke; these commodities were too expensive. However, one corner of the wash-house was called a coal-bunker, but that was a joke. The only other fitment was a chipped stone sink, about two feet long by eighteen inches wide and four inches deep. It had a single cold-water tap and this was our only water supply. With the exception of Gran, we all had to wash ourselves at that sink, even in winter. Gran had a bucket of water and a bowl in her room.

Between the wash-house and the house proper, there was a passage about a yard wide. At the end of the passage, opposite the wash-house door, was the door to the house. This passage caused problems if anyone died as the coffin had to either be stood on end and carried out, or taken through the window. It then had to be carried the length of the court out into Bargate Street and then into the hearse. Most of the hearses of that time were horse-drawn. I still think the horse-drawn hearses, with the black horses wearing plumes on their bridles and the driver on his box, and the bearers walking by the side, looked more impressive than cars. When a cortège passed in those days, people stopped to show respect and men removed their hats. How different things are now, when you see cars nipping in-between hearse and mourners.

Now, to describe our house. Like the others in the court, it was three storeys high. The downstairs room was both living room and kitchen, and went from the front to the back of the house. There was only one window, which was at the front. As we had no gas or electricity, the back of the room was always pretty dark. There was a big black stove, which had an oven and plenty of room for pots on top. Of course, the posh name for it was the 'kitchen range'. It was my mother's pride and joy. She used to black-lead it and shine it every day. She was also proud of her big oil lamp, which had double burners. Most of the neighbours had only single burners or candles.

On the left side of the room were the stairs, which went up to the first floor. There was a small landing, then more stairs to the top floor. Each of the upstairs rooms was supposed to have a wooden partition across the middle, but these were knocked out because there was only one window per floor. There was another reason for knocking the wooden partitions out, which I will explain later.

My grandmother lived on the first floor, in the 'middle room', as we called it. She had a small grate in this room on which she did everything - including her cooking and even boiling her washing. Everything was always spotless. Her bed was separated from her living room by a curtain and the only illumination was a candle. She was so independent; she even papered her room with paper out of the wallpaper pattern books. She thought it looked lovely. For paste, she used flour and water. This was not like modern paste; it really stuck and the bugs loved it!

In her room, my grandmother used to tell me about the First World War. She described the times when the Zeppelins flew over Southampton, and how she and my mother hid under the bed for safety. They were lucky the aerial bombs were quite small then - unlike the ones to come in the not too distant future. My father was at sea at the time. He was in the Dardanelles on the hospital ship, SS *Valdivia*. He was later invalided out with a double rupture caused by lifting wounded soldiers.

The top room of the house was where the rest of the family slept. Again, a curtain divided the room. In the front part, my mother, father and my youngest brother slept. Behind the curtain, at the rear, were one double bed and one single bed. My elder brother and I shared the double and my sister had the single. There was a rear window, about five feet long by one foot. The window was tight to the ceiling. The windowsill was on the top of the back wall of the house, which is still one of the old city walls running down Bargate Street. Recently, this wall was made a feature of a walkway and is now one of the city's tourist attractions. When you walk along it, you are walking on our old windowsills. When I look at this wall now, I find it hard to believe I was born there, as were most of my brothers and my sister.

Now, let me tell you why the wooden partitions were taken down and explain why all the bedsteads were made of iron: The simple reason was that all the houses were infested with bed bugs – whose favourite diet was us! One of my earliest memories is seeing Father in his shirt and long johns, equipped with a candlestick and a big safety pin. He used the safety pin to impale the little horrors. He would go over the bedroom walls very methodically, spearing the horrible little blighters as he went, then would burn them in the flame of the candle. I can still remember how they used to splutter and pop. You daren't crush them because they were full of blood and, besides making a horrible mess, made a terrible smell. Periodically we de-bugged the house using sulphur candles. The neighbours had to de-bug at the same time because, if they didn't, they would get a double helping of bugs as the crafty little pests would just go into their house. Although our neighbours were poor, they were clean and, on the whole, very house-proud. The bugs were just part of our inheritance.

Using sulphur candles was the only method we had to fumigate. Bugs do not like sulphur. The first time we used these candles, we cleared the bugs from our own house, but what we didn't know was that our little friends crawled through the old wall at the back and crept into our neighbours' houses on either side. Soon, dozens of bugs

This is a photo of my Uncle Henry and his son; they were both ships' firemen (stokers). Both served through the First and Second World Wars. While on shift in the stoke hold they were not allowed to smoke, the reason being the atmosphere was full of coal dust and a lighted match would have ignited the dust and blown the ship up. Instead of smoking the men had a stick of 'hard', which was, compressed tobacco, which they chewed like gum. This caused them to produce a lot of saliva, which they spat out in a stream. They also used snuff, which also had to be got rid of by blowing their nose using thumb and finger to hold their nose. Some still chewed when ashore and that was one of the reasons pubs put sawdust on their floors. My uncle signed on for the Titanic but had a premonition that the ship would sink. He jumped ship just before she sailed.

were dropping off their ceilings and walls and there was all hell to pay. So, after that first little episode, everyone debugged at the same time.

Our houses in Tower Place had always been occupied by seafaring families and dockworkers and this is the reason they had bugs. Let me explain: Until the advent of large passenger boats and unions, men wanting to go to sea had to supply their own blankets, eating utensils, plate, mug, and, in some cases, food. Most of the ships, and especially the old wooden ones, were infested with all types of nasty bugs including lice and cockroaches. Many were also infested with rats. Even if a ship sank, then was recovered after a few weeks, the bugs would reappear. Their eggs can lay dormant for years, so, as you can see, when a seaman came home, he brought his kit in his old kit bag complete with its compliment of bugs and lice. That is how the homes became infested.

Incidentally, I have gone into the galleys of some of the biggest liners in the world at night, switched on the lights and the kitchens were alive with cockroaches that disappeared within seconds of the lights coming on. These ships were fumigated every trip but this was to no avail as the eggs would hatch out between fumigations. Most kitchens of big establishments, both on land or sea, have their compliment of cockroaches even now. Cockroaches are indestructible. Now I'm sure you understand why I said that our unwelcome guests were inherited!

3

SCHOOL LIFE

Until it was time for us to go to school at the age of five, we rarely left the court. We played in perfect safety in that little court. Not even a cycle came into the court. Who could afford such a luxury? Everyone walked to work, to school and to the shops. A new cycle cost three or four pounds, which, in most cases for the poor, meant at least two weeks' wages. Of course, this was a time of high unemployment. The Great War had sapped the nation's wealth, and economic recovery was still a long way off. The people most affected by the poor economy were the working class who, in most cases, were living on the bread line.

Five years of age and off to school you went. None of this, 'Go for a couple of hours to get used to it.' Some children were lucky; their mothers took them for their first morning. Mum was not allowed to stop and see you settled in. Even if you screamed the place down, you were taken to your class and that was it. Often, an older brother or sister took the children to school as, in most cases, their mothers had still smaller children at home.

There were no nursery schools in those days. If you were one of the lucky ones, you went home for dinner. From your first day at school you went home with older children. Children tended to go home in their own little groups – e.g. the kids from French Street, Bugle Street, Bargate Street,

Spa Gardens, etc. So you were always in your own little clique. These groups manifested themselves as we got older, when one area would fight another for their own territory. The Chapel or St. Mary's gangs would fight one another, or they would fight the King Street crowd. At the bottom of East Street, where it joins St Mary's Street, there used to be a monument with a horse trough. This was in the middle of St. Mary's Street and this was what we always fought over. Gangs of about 30 or 50 faced one another and hurled abuse. One gang would charge, waving sticks and screaming like banshees and the other gang would retreat, leaving their attackers with the monument. The winners would stay until the losers plucked up enough courage to counter attack. Rarely was anyone seriously hurt and everyone dispersed quickly if a policeman appeared on the scene.

The Bargate and French Street gangs were more spectacular than most. They fought for possession of the "Forty Steps", as we knew them. These are the steps that lead from the top of the old walls down to Western Esplanade. Just imagine hordes of screaming youngsters fighting for possession of the steps!

The French Street gang always had the advantage over us because they gathered at the top of the steps. For us to attack with sticks and stones raining down on us was quite hair-raising. Of course it was not all one-sided. We would throw stones and, in some cases, fire arrows from home-made bows. I can't remember anyone being seriously hurt. The next day we would sit next to one another in class, friend and foe, but all pals again until the next time.

I went to York Buildings School. It was a small school, split into three parts; Infants, Girls, and Boys. The pupils numbered, at the most, three or four hundred. You stayed in the Infants until you were seven or eight years old, then you went up to the 'Big Boys' or 'Big Girls', which were standards three, four, five, six, seven and x-seven. Not all pupils reached x-seven, only the brightest. If you passed your exams you could go on to a Secondary School, like King Edward's. Most of the boys who became eligible could not go, as their parents could not afford to keep them for the extra two years, or supply their school uniform, PE kit, etc. The pupils who went to York Buildings School came from the poorest parts of the town, like the King Street and Ditches (lower Canal Walk) areas, French Street, Bugle Street, Castle Lane, Bargate Street, Tower Place and Spa Road.

Many of the children's parents were dead. There were children of ten years old and upwards who had lost seafaring fathers, brothers and other relatives when the *Titanic* foundered. Others had lost their fathers in the Great War and others may have lost both parents, plus brothers and sisters, in the terrible influenza epidemic which followed the war. In a lot of cases children were brought up by grandparents, aunts, or elder sisters. Some were brought up in Council Homes.

Times were hard for the poorest children then. To see them go to school would shock present-day parents. There were boys wearing father's old hand-me-downs, such as trousers cut off to fit a lad's shorter legs. In some cases, they were not even hemmed, just left ragged. Shirts were 'Dad's old one' or, if not a shirt, an old woolly jumper covered in holes. It was nothing to see a lad with his shirttail poking out of his trouser leg or through the holes in the seat of his pants. In the winter, some were lucky enough to have one of Dad's old jackets with the sleeves rolled up and the bottom of the coat nearly touching the ground. Underwear was unheard of. Quite a lot of lads had no shoes or boots. If they were lucky enough to have footwear, they would have no socks and the shoes would probably have half-crown-sized holes in the soles and string for laces.

Southampton Council eventually issued free boots, but many boys came back to school the next day without them; their parents had taken the boots to the Pawn Shop to get money to buy food, but in some cases it was to buy the father's beer. The Council overcame this problem by stamping the inside of each boot and ordering the pawnbrokers not to take them.

School meals were very different in those days. At twelve o'clock, children could go to 'The Ditches'. It had a kitchen where, I believe, the girls went for cooking lessons. There, you could get a bowl of soup, a slice of bread and a cup of cocoa or tea for one or two old pence. Those who could not afford the meals had free tokens given to them. For some, that was the only food they had all day.

Although times were hard, on the whole, school days were not bad. At least when the weather was bad, you were in the dry and stayed fairly warm. Discipline was firm but fair. The cane was used if you misbehaved and (providing it was not you on the receiving end) you didn't mind.

Each teacher had his own technique with the way he administered his cane. Mr. West would tell you to hold your hand out, then, with the tip of his cane, he would slowly position your hand into the desired position before administering the stroke. The waiting was as bad as the punishment; especially if you had more than one stroke. Mr. McDonald favoured a long ruler, which he used on your knuckles. Mr. Knee just got on with it, but Mr. Collins, who was normally a really nice teacher who rarely used the cane, was an artist when he did. He preferred a long whippy cane. You stood in front of him with your hand out, while

Standard Five, Northam Girls 1926. These girls would have worn their best dresses for the photo.

Southampton school children. The smaller children sitting, most in fancy dress. This was to commemorate King George Fifth Jubilee.

he flexed his cane making it whistle. Then, he would measure you up for the blow. If you had a strong nerve you would leave your hand out to receive the blow. It really hurt, but if you pulled your hand back, that is where his skill came into force. The cane would fly past your fingers and he would immediately make a small adjustment and whip the cane across the back of your fingers. He was a wizard and he was one master I did not upset!

I laugh when I hear or read of people who say the cane is not a deterrent, it certainly was where Mr. Collins was concerned. As a class we all kept his skill down to a minimum. With him, we were the best-behaved class in the school!

There was a brewery opposite our school in York Buildings. The school was named after the road. York Buildings linked Hanover Buildings and East Street. Running across the road was part of the old town walls with an arch over the road, which allowed horses and carts and private cars to pass through. Nothing bigger could pass, so all of the big brewer's drays had to enter from East Street and leave the same way. When the wind was in the right direction, the smell of the brewing beer wafted right through the school. Although we got used to the smell, the effect was to make us feel hungry, so, for some of the lads who had not eaten breakfast, it must have been terrible.

We were lucky to have Southampton's finest sports and playing field in Hoglands Park; the girls and infants had a small, enclosed playground, part of which was the school's basement. The boys had no playground, so, twice a day, we were marched in double file through the arch of York Buildings, across the road at Hanover Buildings and into the Hoglands Park – where the bigger boys played in one area and the smaller boys in another. At the end of games the whistle went, everyone fell into his or her respective class and we marched back to school. When it rained, we just sat in class and talked.

The two youngest classes were lucky to have separate classrooms. The rest of the school was just one big room with drawn curtains to separate the classes. During lessons you really had to concentrate because you had three or four teachers talking at the same time. If a lad was called out for punishment, it really distracted everyone.

I remember one case in particular. A lad in class seven, Jim, was punished and then made to stand in a corner. The master was the headmaster, Mr Weady. Each morning, Mr Weady changed his suit for an older one, as he didn't like to go home with chalk on his clothes. By chance, where Jim was standing in the corner, he was facing the headmaster's suit. He pulled a penknife from his pocket and very expertly cut down the seams of the suit. When it was time to go home, Jim was dismissed with the rest of the class.

The next morning, after prayers, all the curtains were pulled back and Jim was called to the front of the class. He was laid across a desk where other masters held him down while the headmaster delivered the punishment. It was not with a cane but with a leather strap that had been cut into strips. Jim was the only boy I ever saw get the strap. I thought it would kill him, but not Jim; he was as tough as nails. He didn't complain to his parents because he knew it would do no good, as they would only have told him that he got what he deserved. Eventually, Jim went to borstal. He was the hero of Tower Place. All us younger boys worshipped him.

Sports were fun at school. We used to play cricket in the cricket parks and football in Queen's Park, below Edwin Jones (now Debenhams). Because a lot of boys had no boots,

Myself (right) with Tom Ains-worth, he was Southampton Boys' wicket keeper. He also served on Queen Mary from day one and through the War.

the school had a supply of old football boots – the old leather ones with hard toecaps and leather studs. Those were old boots that had never seen dubbin and, in most cases, had missing studs or no studs at all. There were never enough boots to go around, so you usually had just one boot to play in which you tied on with string.

Being thus equipped for football, we were marched down to the parks. We must have looked a sight – some with one bare foot and, on the other foot, an old football boot tied with string. Some boys had patched trousers, ragged jerseys or coats that had belonged to Dad or the lodger. Some had caps with holes through which their hair poked out. Little did we know that, in a few years time, we lads would be fighting and dying for our country, the same as our fathers had done before us.

The sports fun began when we got to the parks, especially if it was a Monday, because that was washing day. The women who lived in the area all used one end of the park to hang out their washing. They lived mostly in the little cuts off East Street; some lived as far as the Kings Street area. There were no spin dryers in those days, only mangles

- if you could afford one. If not, women had to wring the clothes by hand. There was no nylon; everything was either cotton or wool. Silk clothes were for the rich.

Imagine carrying a galvanised iron or steel bath, full of washing, up to a quarter of a mile to hang it out to dry. God only knows what weight some of the women carried. These women were the great-grandmothers of the present generation. Quite a few of them were killed during the Second World War, when the bomb shelters they were in received direct hits by bombs.

As boys, we often kicked our muddy old footballs into the washing lines. To us it was fun, but how those women must have cursed us!

I was at school for most of the twenties and one more example of how children lived in those days stands out in my memory. A boy in my class had to sit on his own because he nearly always smelt strongly of urine and no one would sit next to him. He himself was embarrassed, but could do nothing about it. He belonged to a large family who lived in just two rooms. The children slept on a mattress; girls one end, boys the other. As he was the eldest, it was his job to look after the baby and it slept next to him. The baby used to wet the bed and of course the poor blighter's shirt also got wet. He had to wear the shirt he slept in to school the next day. The terrible thing was, he had to sleep on the urine soaked mattress every night. The only coverings on the bed were old coats and whatever else could be found. No sheets, blankets or pillows for them; they were poor and no one cared. Animals were better treated. Those impoverished people were products of the 'Great British Empire'.

Not all children at York Buildings School were like the ones mentioned above. Some were fairly well off, like Bert

Knott, whose father was a fish merchant, and Blanchard, who had an antique shop in Below Bar. Then there were the Powell brothers, whose father was landlord of The Platform public house. These lads and a few others went on to higher education at King Edward's. The other boys' fathers (if they had one) were bait diggers, shipyard workers, stevedores, or they worked in the merchant navy.

The children in our family were luckier than most – we had two summer holidays! After the official six-week school holiday ended in August, we went hop picking with other families. Each September, we spent three weeks picking hops at Wheatlea Farm in Bentley, Hampshire, and near Alton.

At the appointed hour, everyone turned up at the West Station (now Southampton Central). What a motley horde we were!

There were the Smiths from Northam. Poor Mrs. Smith lost her son Sonny when he swallowed a balloon and choked to death. The popular song of the day was, 'Sonny Boy', and we kids were not allowed to sing it because it made Mrs. Smith cry. Then there were the Greenwoods. Mrs Greenwood was a widow with a grown-up family. They all used to come: Rachel, Kate, Charlie, Henry and two of their mates. All the men were stokers and trimmers on the boats. A real tough crew, but to us kids they were a bunch of softies. Then there were the Buttons, a really poor family. My Aunt Clara also came with some of her family – she had fifteen children. All but one, Violet, are dead now. Aunt Clara's younger children – Stella, Bill Fred, Dot and Nellie came 'hopping'. There were two more families who came hop picking with us, but I have forgotten their names.

We all gathered on the platform with our bags, pots, pans, kettles, blankets, various boxes and sacks, everything but the kitchen sink. The train took us to Bentley Halt, where everything had to be taken off and loaded onto a heavy four-wheeled wagon pulled by a pair of shire horses. Small children were loaded on top of the luggage and everyone else walked the mile and half to the farm, all happy and singing. Our destination was a row of simple huts – it was like coming home as everyone went to the hut they had used the previous year.

After offloading, wooden faggots were laid on the floor on one side of the hut. Palliasses were then filled with straw and laid on the faggots. That was our bed. Everyone slept on the same bed except for the Greenwood men who had their own hut. Whilst the beds were being prepared, fires were lit on the ground outside and kettles were put on to boil.

The next day you were allocated your picking position and given your tally book. When the whistle blew, there were loud cheers and the first vines were pulled. Hop picking had started! You were paid by the bushel and four times a day the hops were measured and the amount entered in your tally book. The work continued until every field was cleared. We always prayed for good weather. The children always had a lovely time; not picking many hops but having a lot of fun picking blackberries and scrumping apples.

Saturday was shopping day. All the men took a sub from their earnings and went off to the pub as did the men from all the other farms, and many of the women joined them. Everyone was flush with money. It was usually dark by the time everyone got back to the farm. The boys had been busy carving out mangels – cutting out scary eyes, noses and mouths. They would wait for their parents to get back to light candles and put them inside the mangels. When the women came by they shrieked and yelled, pretending to be frightened. When all the fires were stoked up, we sang and danced by the flickering flames.

My Cousin Stella's boyfriend once rode his bike up for the weekend with his piano accordion on his back. He played and people sang while Stella danced her dagger dance, flashing her knife, which glinted in the dark. Round and round the fire she went then, suddenly, she danced right through the burning embers. Sparks flew all over the place. Everyone gasped and then cheered. She was unharmed.

On the last Sunday evening a door was removed from one of the huts and, with poles driven into the ground, it was made into a table. Two large poles were then driven into the ground and a sheet tied between them to make a screen. A small group of men and women arrived with a large magic lantern (early projector). This was placed on the table. A paraffin lamp was placed inside and lit. Everyone grouped round facing the screen and we had a service. The hymns were flashed on the screen. One of the group played a foot pump organ and another, who had a pointer, followed the words. Everyone sang. For most of them it was their only church service of the year.

The last day of hop picking was the reverse of the first day. As the last vine was pulled, everyone cheered. Everyone went to the farm to collect his or her earnings and we all travelled home. Hop picking (and our holiday) was over for another year.

My Uncle Jim in his old Model T Ford truck, which was driven by his son Henry, met Aunt Clara at the station. My dad had a pony and cart. All the rest of the hoppers had to trek across Southampton carrying their pots, pans and bits and pieces. The likes of the 'hoppers' coming home will never be seen again. Children's voices will never again echo over the hop fields of England. The only sound there today is that of the tractor.

4

ST MICHAEL'S AND BUCKLES

The walled city of Southampton – the area that is now the lower part of the town centre, is filled with buildings of historical interest. Council houses were first built in Upper Bugle Street in the early twenties. A couple of these still exist and are preserved as protected buildings. They are occupied and are located next to the Juniper Berry public house. Further down Bugle Street were several other buildings of interest – the first council flats to be built in the town and St. Michael's House, a large lodging house for down and outs. Although these are now demolished, many remember them.

Also in Bugle Street, next to the Tudor House, runs a cut called Blue Anchor Lane. Even now, a walk down Blue Anchor Lane is a nostalgic experience – at least it is to me. The lane starts in Bugle Street, runs along the side of the Tudor House and gardens to an archway, which is built into the old city walls, and ends on Western Esplanade. The path is paved with old-fashioned paving stones from an age long gone. When I was a boy, the lane held another attraction to the children of the area. Overhanging the garden of Tudor House is a very old mulberry tree. We used to throw sticks up at the tree to bring the ripe berries down and scramble for them as they fell. Our fingers and mouths were blue in no time but no one cared because the fruit tasted so lovely.

I should think this is the only mulberry tree in the walled city of Southampton and if you walk down Blue Anchor Lane even now when the fruit is ripe, the paving stones beneath the tree are stained blue from the juice of the fallen fruit. I wonder how many generations of local children have eaten the fruit of the Tudor House mulberry tree? I must admit I visited Tudor House a couple of years ago when the fruit was ripe and picked and ate a berry, just for old time's sake.

Opposite Blue Anchor lane stood St. Michael's lodging house. It was a large house that catered for the tramps and destitute people of the town, where, for a few pence, they could obtain a bed for the night. It was run by the Council and was supervised by a warden. There were primitive facilities for washing, hot water for drinks and recreation and rest rooms.

The men who used St. Michael's had to book beds on a first-come, first-served, basis. Some of the occupants were regulars; others were just passing through. A warden was on duty twenty-four hours a day and everyone had to be in by a certain time – I think it was half-past ten at night. Rules were strictly kept and drunkards and troublemakers were severely dealt with.

Unwary occupants of St Michael's could wake up in the morning and find their boots or other possessions missing. This did not happen to the regulars; when they took their boots off, they lifted the end of the bed and placed their boots with a leg of the bed in each one, thus foiling any would-be thief. They would then put the rest of their clothes beneath the mattress. If they had valuables, they lodged them with the warden until morning. The vicar of St. Michael's Church and the Roman Catholic priest of St.

Joseph's Church had a certain number of free tickets to St Michael's House, which they gave to really destitute vagrants. These were for one night only and were given very sparingly.

In St. Michael's Square there was a general shop called Buckles which baked its own bread and cakes. It also sold coal, oil, fruit, vegetables, groceries and a certain amount of haberdashery. Besides catering for the local residents, Buckles was a Godsend to the occupants of the lodging house, who would come in and buy such items as a penny screw of tea (a small amount of tea put in a newspaper cone which was then screwed or twisted. Sugar was treated in the same way), a small tin of condensed milk, half a loaf of bread or a penny piece of cheese. Butter and margarine were bought by the ounce. The St Michael's House customers were treated with as much respect as someone who had spent a pound. Sadly, Buckles, like other small shops of their type, was forced out of business by the superstores that don't cater for people who need only small amounts. Such is progress.

St. Michael's lodging house was closed and demolished in the late 'fifties. In its place we now have a 'cardboard city' and you'll find down-and-outs sleeping in abandoned cars and derelict buildings. Society was more caring in the twenties.

The town also had what we called The Poorhouse. This was a large building next to St. Mary's Church. It catered for the destitute men and women of the town plus others who were passing through. A tramp, or someone looking for work, could stay there if they had no money. They were expected to do a certain amount of work for their bed and board, and this is why it was commonly called The Workhouse. The permanent residents were provided with a dark grey suit that was made of a very course material. You would often see a couple of the men walking along the edge of the pavements looking for cigarette ends or 'dog ends' as they called them. If a cigar end was found, it was considered a bonus. Goodness knows what types of diseases were passed on by this practice.

5

LIFE AS IT WAS

A lot of boys supplemented their food by begging. They would go to the dock gates, or Pirelli's, when the workers came out and say, "Any bread left mister?" Some of the men saved part of their lunch for the beggars – normally bread and margarine, sometimes a bit of cheese and, if the boys were lucky, a bit of cake. These boys guarded their pitches outside the gates against all-comers. If they were handed too much for themselves, they gave the rest to other boys. Nothing was wasted and, of course, they kept the best for themselves.

Southampton was a pretty rough town in the twenties and thirties, and especially so at weekends. East Street, The Strand, The Ditches and Orchard Lane, were often the scenes of drunken fights. The police were tall, tough men who usually had the job of breaking up these fights and, up to a point, they seemed to enjoy it.

Most policemen were ex-service men. If a man was knocked unconscious, as sometimes happened, he would be wheeled to Bargate Police Station on a pair of hand trucks borrowed from Smith the Coal Merchant, in Orchard Lane, or in a taxi (first horse-drawn, later motor).

When the *Leviathan*, an American ship, came in, the crew would come ashore to get drunk. Prohibition meant the USA was a dry country, so the poor old 'Yanks' really went to town when they came ashore. The result was always trouble in a big way. The police showed them no mercy and often used truncheons on them. As we lived in Bargate Street, we were used to seeing taxis pull up at the police station. Two or three policemen would climb out and drag anything up to four or five semi-conscious or unconscious sailors from the floor of the taxi. The next morning they would be up before the beak at the Bargate Magistrates Court, fined and sent back to their ship.

This system of justice was still in force in 1938, but was stopped after an American visitor tripped on the tramlines opposite the Royal Pier. He fell in the road and a policeman thought he was a seaman. He hit him with his baton and whipped him off to the police station, where it was discovered the man was an American lawyer. The case was in all the national papers. I actually read about it in India. I do not know what happened to the policeman.

The town police did not wear helmets in the twenties and thirties. Instead, they wore military-style caps, like an army red cap, except it was blue and had a white cover on it. If they had worn helmets like they do today, it is possible the helmets would have been knocked from their heads and used as weapons. In the scuffles they had, anything went – except I don't remember a knife being used. It wasn't the done thing. Only 'Dagos' used knives.

The single form of transport for a policeman in pre-war years was a bicycle. These were used mostly by the sergeants when visiting policemen on the beat. All the patrolling was done on foot and that is why policemen were called 'flat-feet'. They had no walkie-talkies, only a whistle. If a policeman needed assistance, he blew his whistle. It would usually be heard by another policeman, who would then blow his whistle and they would run to one another's assistance. Of course, everyone else heard the whistles and quite a few would also run just to see what was going on, which, in some cases, was of great help to the policeman in trouble. If a policeman was in trouble, help came from all directions.

There was another type of man who patrolled the town. He was the dreaded School Board man. Any child caught during school times on the road or 'round the shops' would be stopped, questioned, returned to school and duly punished. If you were off school, the School Board man came to your home and your mother had to give a good reason for your absence. If a child continued to be absent, the parents were taken to court and fined.

There was an 'evil' we did not have in the twenties and thirties – that was delivery charges. If you bought anything it was delivered free: papers, bread, milk. Furniture delivery charges were unheard of. A letter cost one-and-a-half old pence to post. Christmas cards and such cost a penny to post if the envelope was not stuck down but tucked inside. There was only one class of post, no first or second class, and the postmen made up to three deliveries a day. They were never late. I can see the postman now with his funny hat, which had a peak at the front *and* one at the back. The idea was, if it was raining and he bent his head to look at the mail, the rain did not run down his neck.

Another man I used to love to watch was the lamp lighter, who rode his bike, armed with a long cane that had a metal hook on the end. He zigzagged down the road from one side to the other, turning the streetlights on or turning them off without getting off his bike or stopping. He was a joy to watch; cane poised as he approached the lamppost. A little flick and the light was on. I never saw him miss once. Now, one flick and the whole town lights up!

When I was about eleven, one of our neighbours died. She was a big person and, as I have already explained, our houses were not built with comfort in mind. They could not get the body down the stairs because they were too narrow and if they had gone part way, they couldn't turn, so it had to go through the bedroom window. The window had to be taken out and the body was maneuvered through it with the help of a block and tackle and lowered to the ground. All the women in the court were upset because everyone turned out to watch. They all solemnly paid their respects, but to the children it was great fun to watch.

At a funeral in those days, black was the order of the day. Even the poorest of the poor tried to wear black, even if it meant pawning their most prized possessions to do so. As a last resort they would even pawn their wedding rings. No one wore brown boots to a funeral – if you only had brown boots, you stained them black. The men wore a black cap and a black neckerchief. Not many poor people wore ties. They also wore a black armband or sewed a black diamond on the sleeve of their coat. These were supposed to be worn for six months. The women wore black dresses or skirts and blouses (often borrowed). If they were lucky, they had a black coat, if not, they wore a black shawl. Some women had a black hat and some hats even had a black ostrich feather on them. If this was the case, it was used over and over again because a woman really felt someone if she could sport that kind of a hat at a funeral.

Our nearest public house was The Arundel at the bottom of Bargate Street where the men folk and, if they were flush, their womenfolk, went for a drink. You would often see women go into The Bottle and Jug with a jug under their pinny or their shawl to get half a shoot for 'the old man'. This cost two old pennies, just under one pence decimal. A woman may also buy her husband two Woodbine cigarettes for a penny. (The landlord used to gain one cigarette out of every packet of five by selling them this way, which meant an extra halfpenny profit on a packet). Even a farthing (value quarter of a penny) was worth something then. Children could buy a gobstopper (a large round sweet) for a farthing.

The High Street, or at least Above Bar, was paved with wooden blocks the same size as a house brick. These were sprayed with tar. The tramlines, which ran up and down the middle of the road, had cobbles between them because, prior to them being electrified, horses had pulled the trams and the cobbles gave them a better grip and did not wear out so quickly.

Some families could not afford a coal fire, so they used to scrounge anything to burn; scrap wood, cardboard, kitchen waste etc. One morning, council workers started digging up the wood blocks from the street prior to resurfacing the road with the newly discovered tarmacadam. The wood blocks were to be dumped, but as soon as they were dug up, men, women and children grabbed them. People came from all over town with sacks, pushchairs, prams, wheelbarrows - anything in which to carry away the blocks.

The blocks were made from red pine but, as they were covered in tar, the number of chimney fires rapidly increased. This caused problems because if a fire engine turned up, they put the hose down the chimney and, besides putting out the fire, they also flooded the room the fire was in. It was bad enough if the fire was in the downstairs room, but a lot of houses had families living upstairs (overcrowding being the norm in those days). The more families, the more rent for the landlord.

In Bargate Street, one house had at least five families in,

all with children, and had only one door to the street. So, if a chimney from one of the top rooms caught fire and the firemen came and put the hose down that chimney, the water went right through the house bringing down ceilings and flooding all the rooms. In the twenties and thirties very few people had fire insurance (they barely had enough money for food), so if this happened to them it was a major catastrophe. The town council or government offered no help and they had to carry on as best they could. For this reason, the fire services were not called until all other efforts failed, or some other public-spirited citizen called it for them – heaven help him if the householder found out who the caller was.

Chimney fires could be very dangerous, especially if the chimney was very dirty. If it was a very bad fire, flames would shoot out of the chimney pot making it so hot it would shatter. Burning clinkers of soot would fall into the grate where the poor, unfortunate householder was frantically putting burning soot into a bucket or bowl, trying to prevent burning embers from coming into the room and setting the rest of the house on fire.

Salt was used to help kill a fire. If you were lucky enough to put the fire out yourself, the room would be in a terrible state afterwards – what with the smoke and soot. Fortunately, neighbours helped one another to clear everything up.

The reason I have described a chimney fire in detail is that this type of fire was happening all over Southampton – caused by the people who were burning the tarred blocks they had taken from the road works in Above Bar. The situation became so serious that a policeman was posted to prevent the removal of further blocks.

Smokeless zones did not exist in the twenties. In winter,

smoke belched from houses and factories. It also belched from the ships in the docks. When there was no wind, the smoke could not disperse and the town was covered with black smog or fog. Visibility was often down to a few yards, and sometimes, a few feet. Tuberculosis (TB) was then a common, almost incurable disease and numerous sufferers of TB died during the foggy periods of the winter months – amongst them, young babies and children.

6

EVENTS OF THE TWENTIES, PLUS!

In the early twenties, there was an outbreak of rabies in Britain. Countless animals, including birds (both wild and tame), had to be slaughtered in the affected areas. All dogs had to be muzzled.

I did not realise what a terrible disease rabies was until, while in India during the war, one of our lads was nipped by an eight-week-old puppy and he contracted rabies. He died a terrible death, just like a wild animal. I hope they never relax the quarantine laws of this country because, even today, it is rare for anyone who has contracted this disease to survive.

During the summers of the twenties, the Royal Pier, with its brightly coloured dome and flags, was a very popular place. There were various stalls to the left of the entrance, where people sold fruit and there was Rocky Joe Saunders with his home-made sweets stall. There were also novelties and penny balloons for sale. People used to cram into the pier area. Trams carried people in from outlying districts of the town and trains arrived at the pier full of visitors. The trams drove on to the end of the pier allowing passengers to transfer to paddle steamers, which went to Southsea and the Isle of Wight.

Many people came to visit Southampton. They often came

in 'charabancs' (coaches), some of which had solid rubber tyres. The pier area was always crowded during the holidays.

The area opposite the pier, where the Mayflower Memorial stands, was very popular with children. There were two rows of old canons - relics from one of the wars. The front row was of large canons, the second row, which was on the walled walkway at the back, contained only small guns. Children loved playing on them. Some sat on the barrels of the guns, whilst others pretended to fire them. While the children played, parents sometimes nipped into the local pubs for 'a quick one' or went to the shellfish stall for a plate of cockles. The guns were taken away for salvage during the Second World War.

Another popular place to visit was the tower known as The Penny Balloon. The walls and the tower always had crowds of people with children on them. Many of the children had penny balloons and, as it was usually breezy on top, the children often let their balloons go. If the wind was in the right direction, the balloons floated across Southampton Water. Of course, to the west, there were no new docks at that time, so you had uninterrupted views of the River Test estuary and the New Forest. Sometimes, balloons were released on purpose to have a race. It was nothing to see several balloons floating over Southampton Water, often to cheers and sometimes to tears.

Looking up from the ground to the tower and the battlements on a busy, sunny day you could see dozens of coloured balloons and waivers (coloured streamers on sticks) - a sight that has gone forever.

In a stretch of water between the town quay and the docks was the world's largest floating dry dock. To see it submerge and then see the largest ocean liners in the world

- My Southampton -

manoeuvered into it was quite a sight. Air would then be blown into its ballast tanks and the liner would rise up with water pouring from its sides. The well-known ships of the day, to name but a few, were the *Mauritania*, the *Aquitania* and the *Majestic Olympic*, which was the sister ship of the *Titanic*.

The permanent King George the Fifth Dry Dock was built in later years for larger ships like the *Queen Mary*, that were too big for the floating dock. The floating dock eventually went to the Far East.

There was no New Docks in the twenties and, although there were plenty of ships, dockworkers were mainly casual. Men used to walk from places like Romsey, Totton and the New Forest and, on the other side, from as far as Titchfield, Fareham. To try to get work, they had to line up in front of a foreman, who would select the men he wanted. The foreman's mates were always chosen first (the 'blue eyes', as they were called). Those that did not get selected for work in the morning had to wait for the midday pick-up. If they still did not get selected, home they went and returned the next day to try again.

It was rumoured that, if you had a pretty young wife and were prepared to close your eyes, you would always get work. Those men were treated more like slaves than free men.

Work began to get a little better in the late twenties. This was when council estates were built: Coxford, The Flower Gardens, Swaythling, Shirley Warren, and Merry Oak. Suddenly, families who had been living in one room, with maybe two or three children, were given a brand new house. Imagine, hardly any furniture, separate bedrooms for themselves and the children, a kitchen, a bathroom, hot water from a back boiler, a front and rear garden and gas and electric! Some families had only ever used candles or oil lamps.

It was at this time that hire-purchase took off. It was heaven, but like all things, the goods still had to be paid for. The lucky families were those with seamen who were on the American run. In 1920, Prohibition was declared in the 'States. Alcohol became illegal and the American gangsters like Al Capone became smugglers on a grand scale. Everyone wanted illegal 'hooch' and the price of a bottle of whisky, gin or brandy went through the roof. This proved a heaven-sent gift for British seamen in two ways. First, they smuggled in and sold a few bottles of alcohol each trip. Then, with the money from their sales they bought things that were impossible to get at home, such as jeans and elaborate leather belts with fancy buckles and bright glass stones. Once home, they sold their purchases at a reasonable profit. It was not long before you saw the young men of the town swanking around with 'Yankee' jeans and belts. The jeans had two back pockets with copper rivets on each side and two front pockets, again with rivets. The pockets were patch pockets with white seam stitching, as were the trousers, with a double white seam up the trouser leg. When they were new, you could stand them up. With the profits from their sales, most of the family men furnished their houses. Prohibition, which lasted until 1933, was a boon to Southampton, Liverpool and other seaports.

There were three other projects, which helped the town's economy. These were the building of the Civic Centre, the Sports Centre and the New Docks.

The Civic Centre was built on what we always called The Marlands. As a lad, I played football there and once went to see a circus there. The Marlands was shaped like a bowl, with banks on some sides. This building of the Civic Centre was attributed to Sir Sidney Kimber. Apparently, one of the stipulations was that the building materials came from Hampshire with the gravel coming from Romsey. However, the contractors felt it did not matter where they got their gravel, so they found a way out of the stipulation by routing all their lorries through Romsey. Their contract said that all gravel should come 'from Romsey' and technically it did.

The second big project was the building of the Sports Centre. This was known as the Mayor's Scheme, as it was his 'baby'. It was a very clever idea. First, you had a core of professional men, then you had a labour force. The labour force was drawn from the mass of unemployed that, on a voluntary basis, worked for no pay but gained points as they worked. It was simple; a man worked so many hours for so many points. The points allowed him to buy items of clothing and food parcels. Soon, there were smart young men walking around town and some not so smart – those who had pawned the proceeds of their labour for beer.

The Sports Centre is the final resting place of a much-loved police horse, Warrior. He lies there minus his hooves, which were removed by George Wilson, the slaughter man, and turned into holders for pens and other knickknacks. One, I believe, went to the Mayor, one to the Chief of Police, one may have gone to PC Strong, whose horse it was, and the other went to the slaughter man, who passed the hoof to his son, who in turn gave it to his daughter, Louisa.

Going down Southampton Water, on the Netley side of the river, in the late twenties, you would have found a line of ships moored stem to stern. They were victims of the depression and were all bound for the scrapyard. One of them was named the *Old Saxon* and her homeport had been Southampton. On the other side of the water a number of flying boats were moored. These went as far as Calshot. Calshot was then a RAF station, where an aircraftsman named J. Shaw sometimes worked. Shaw's real name was T.E. Lawrence - also known as Lawrence of Arabia - one of the great heroes of World War One. With the government's knowledge, he had enlisted in the lower ranks under a false name in order to research a book about enlisted men. Although T.E. Lawrence was in the RAF as a low ranked aircraftsman, he was allowed to come and go as he pleased. Shaw was only interested in the RAF power boats.

T.E. Lawrence lived in Southampton for a while and spent quite a lot of time in Southampton Library, which was then on the corner of Bedford Place and London Road. There, he made friends with a few of the local library users. An old docker, named George (I forget his surname) told me of Lawrence's visits to Southampton Library. George was one of the men who lined up for work at the dock gates every day. If he did not get selected in the morning, he would go to the library, where it was warm and he could read the daily newspapers. This was how he met Lawrence.

George described Lawrence as looking like 'a nobody'. He said he would get a book from the shelves, take notes and put the book back. George had no idea what he was researching. George did not know who Lawrence was at first, but started talking to him and Lawrence explained who he was. George said he was a nice bloke, not stuck up at all. You would never have thought he was Lawrence of Arabia.

Eventually, Lawrence felt the government had let him down by reneging on a promise made to him and the Arab nation. In retaliation, he relinquished all his ranks, even refusing an award of the Victoria Cross. Some felt he was an embarrassment to the government. He later died in a motorcycle accident.

In 1931, I went to Calshot and watched the Schneider Trophy race when Britain, flying uncontested, retained the trophy with a record speed. The aircraft were made by Supermarine in Southampton and were prototypes for our most famous fighter plane, the Spitfire. They were fitted with floats and the pilots were from the RAF.

Before the race, Lady Houston, who had sponsored the 1931 trophy with a donation of a £100,000, gave each pilot some new pennies, which they returned to her after the race. She had the fastest pennies in the world!

Britain had also won the Schneider Trophy in Calshot in 1929. The competing planes that year were Italian... and they were left standing. It was a one-horse race!

Lady Houston had a large yacht anchored on the river. I believe a celebration party, which included all the contestants, was held on board after the race. Lady Houston came from, or lived in, the Channel Islands and was very wealthy. She sponsored the Schneider Trophy race in 1931 because, after the French and Italian teams had to pull out, the British government refused to put up the money. I think we all owe a lot to her because, if she had not sponsored the race, there is a possibility there would have been no Spitfire, and this would have been catastrophic for us during the war that was soon to come.

During the thirties, Calshot was home to one of the country's white elephants. It was the largest flying boat in the world and was called the *Princess*. It had eight engines. It was tested on the river and over the town, but it was found to be underpowered. It could only get up to a few hundred feet. I saw it fly. It is a pity that jet engines had not been invented then, because The *Princess* was a beautiful plane. It stood on the slipway at Calshot for at least two years before it was destroyed.

This period was also the era of the airship: Britain had two and Germany had two. These airships had gondolas attached below their gas-filled balloons and were capable of crossing the Atlantic Ocean with ease. They flew over Southampton as they travelled to and from 'The States'. The British airships had numbers: R100 and R101. The German airships had names. One was the *Hindenberg* the other was the *Graff-Spey*. The German airships had large German crosses painted on them. In a few years time, Sotonians were to see many more aircraft bearing these crosses.

The German airships always seemed to fly lower and slower than our own. We all said that the Germans were taking photographs of the country. I think later events proved us right.

All four airships met tragic ends with tragic loss of life. One, the *Hindenberg*, went up in flames as it landed in America. It was being moored to its docking mast when it caught fire. This horrific event was filmed and shown in cinemas around the world. The gas used to inflate the balloons was helium, which is highly flammable. It was terrible to see so many people lose their lives. England lost an airship that crashed in France, also catching fire and again with great loss of life. The two remaining airships later met the same fate.

7

CHRISTMAS AND NEW YEAR

A t Christmas and New Year no one had much money.
There were more people out of work than in. We were
in the Depression and we had had a general strike.
Amazingly, *students* helped to break that strike. Today, our
impression is that students would be first in line for
industrial action! How times change!

The students drove tramcars, they were conductors, they
were postmen, and, providing they did not have to get their
hands dirty, they did all the jobs that people on strike would
have done. And they were paid for it. This did not endear
them to the ordinary working man.

Following the General Strike, things were hard for the
poor of the town. Pawnshops did a roaring trade and, to
add to it all, the government of the day brought in a 'means
test'. This really hit the poor because, if they applied to the
Council for help, they were visited by a Council person –
complete with clipboard – who would go into their home
and ask questions. The first question was, 'How many live
in the house?' The answer was their guideline. They would
then commence to inspect every item you possessed. If it
was summer and you had two blankets per bed, you were
told you only needed one, so the spare ones had to be
pawned. These inspectors went right through the house.
Everything, except the real essentials, had to go. If you had

five chairs and there were only four of you, one chair had to go, as did pots, pans, crockery, cutlery, jewellery, and every unnecessary, or 'excess' thing you had. *They* decided what was, or was not, excess. You then had to sell all your so-called excess goods and you did not get any monetary help until you had used up the money you received from selling your belongings.

To get back to Christmas; how different it was then! I'll start with schools: weeks before Christmas, parcels and boxes arrived at all the schools in the town and, as the day for breaking-up for Christmas got nearer, more boxes and parcels arrived. We were all at fever pitch by the time the last day of school arrived. No one was absent! The roll was called, prayers were over and children went with their teachers and brought boxes and parcels back to their respective classes. We were told to read quietly while our teacher checked the parcels to see what was in them. He would not let us see. When the bell rang we went out of York Buildings, fell in line and marched to the park for a quarter of an hour, after which we went back to class to finally open the boxes! Everyone laughed aloud, including the master.

The first things to come out were paper carrier bags; everyone received one. Then, out came goodies from various boxes – we would get a small bag of sweets, a bar of chocolate, a pencil, a ruler, paper hats, balloons, colouring books, a small tin (about an inch high) of Ovaltine, just enough for one cup. Every item we received had been donated by various local companies. This scene was being enacted all over the town. A lot of the children had no toys of their own and these bits and pieces were something to treasure. The pleasure we children got from those presents cannot be imagined.

A large proportion of the pupils at my school had lost their fathers on the *Titanic* or in the Great War. Some had also lost their mothers in the influenza epidemic. Even now, I think how lucky I was to have a father and mother whilst I was growing up.

Although the Depression occurred in the twenties, at Christmas-time all the shops were decorated and the big stores, like Edwin Jones, had Christmas grottos, which you paid to go into. Here, children were transported into amazing fairylands filled with animated figures depicting Christmas scenes and fairy tales, and each child received a present from Father Christmas on the way out. East Street had various types of stalls the whole way from All Saints Church to Ganges Shoe Shop at the bottom.

During Christmas week the town was packed with shoppers who came from every outlying district via all sorts of transport. In the early twenties, you saw shooting-brakes (carriages that could carry eight or ten passengers, drawn by a pair of frisky horses), farm carts, horses and traps, and some very shaky old buses, all fully laden with men, women and children, ready to do their Christmas shopping.

There were no car parks in those days, so hotels and inns were used to stable horses in Above Bar. Just above Bargate Street was The George Hotel. For some unknown reason, I have never seen The George mentioned. It had the largest stable and yard in the town, plus a large apple orchard. The George was always used when the circus came to town, when elephants and such were stabled there.

Tom Mix, a famous cowboy actor, performed at the Hippodrome in Southampton and his horse, Tony, was stabled at The George, as was the horse of another famous cowboy actor, Hoot Gibson. I remember going to see Tom Mix at the 'Hip', as we called it. He rode his horse onto the stage, did a couple of tricks on it, then, facing the audience, he made his horse rear and, at the same time, he drew his gun and fired it in the air. The audience loved it.

Let's get back to Christmas shopping! At the end of their day's shopping, people would be laden with their Christmas wares and, having shopped, ate and drank, they were in a merry mood. The horse-drawn vehicles loaded with happy people clutching their bags and parcels and the children with their balloons, all singing as they drove out of the town's hostelries were a happy and colourful sight.

East Street was always packed until late evening during the Christmas period. Carts and carriages (plus the few cars that were around in those times) gave the street a wide berth.

Besides the stalls along East Street, there were always paperboys selling newspapers. The sound of their shouting could be heard for most of the day and evening. The paperboys did not only sell the *Echo*; they could be heard shouting, "Evening News, Star and Standard Echo". Some even shouted the headlines of the day. The stall vendors also shouted their wares.

There were also gypsies selling holly wreaths and mistletoe at Christmas-time. Nearly everyone hung a sprig of mistletoe inside their door. No female could refuse to be kissed under the mistletoe! There was also a man who sold jumping beans from a tray, which hung from a cord around his neck. The beans were real beans that had been imported from South America. To see these beans jump all over his tray was magic! The cost of a jumping bean was a penny. The funny thing was, when you took your bean home it would never jump. What we did not know at the time was that the bottom of the man's tray was made of metal, which he heated with a candle. Each bean had a maggot in it; so, when it was placed on the hot tray it wriggled violently to escape the heat. This made the bean jump. 'Jumping beans' were imported every year and they were legal.

This is Bill my cousin selling bananas and coconuts at a fair. This was about 1938. Bananas were not sold by the pound then but according to size, big ones seven for sixpence, smaller, two a penny.

Christmas Eve was always special. The locals left most of their shopping until the evening and that was the time East Street really came alive. As darkness fell, all the stalls lit their lights. From the top to the bottom of the street you'd see a line of naked flames hissing and roaring away. The street was packed with shoppers and the pubs were all full. As the evening wore on, prices in the various butcher shops dropped and the locals went after the bargains. Misslebrook and Weston always had a big display of poultry, which was drastically reduced the later it got, as did the meat in Northovers butcher's shop. Refrigeration was in its infancy then and most shops did not have freezers. Even shops that did have freezers could not keep large amounts of stock. Most shops had only a room that was kept cold by blocks of ice. Poultry was a delicacy in those days and ordinary people could afford to buy a chicken just once a year.

By about 10 o'clock on Christmas Eve, shoppers began to head home. The pubs closed and the revellers made their way home too. You could see them, arm-in-arm, all across the street – merry men and women loaded with their shopping, all singing carols and dancing as they went. One little ditty that was popular summed it all up. I remember part of it; 'Tired and spent, with my rhubarb all bent, shopping on Saturday night'. It was a catchy little tune. Can you imagine the little groups of people singing and dancing, the oil lamps roaring and smoking, and the smell of paraffin? It was Christmas Eve and everyone was happy.

Come Christmas Day, the church bells rang, but it was otherwise quiet – no cars racing about and no children with new bicycles and expensive toys in those days. Most of the children's toys, if they had any, came from Woolworth's, the new department shop. The price of a toy was usually sixpence. A lot of the things at Woolworth's came from Germany, which was then in a terrible depression. Inflation was out of control over there, making exports very cheap. English children could be seen playing shops with millions of German Marks, as they were then valueless.

If you walked down East Street on Christmas morning there would not be a stall in sight and not a bit of rubbish to be seen. The Council did a good job in those days.

Most houses were overcrowded, with sometimes two, three, or even four families living under one roof. They usually had only one oven between them all. The cooking was done on either a Primus stove or over a small bedroom fire. Because of this, it was at Christmastime that bakers came into their own. For a few pence they would roast your Yuletide dinner. We were lucky in our house – we had the kitchen range that was my mother's pride and joy - always blackleaded and always shining.

My uncle lived at the entrance to Tower Place. His house was in Bargate Street and was built into the Old Walls. Half of his house formed an arch about nine feet wide and about ten feet high, which was the only way into Tower Place. To get to Tower Place we had to go through the arch, which was part of his house.

This is my father's elder brother Jim with his daughter Stella. He was one of the best watercress growers in Hampshire Stella could always be found at the entrance to the common selling flowers on Sundays for people visiting the cemetery. No matter what the weather was like, she was there.

My uncle had a big family and was in business dealing in fruit and flowers and was a grower of watercress. He always had a large turkey for Christmas - too big for his own oven - so the baker's oven in Buckles, in St. Michael's Square, came in handy for him. My aunt used to give me sixpence to take the turkey to the baker's.

One Christmas, when I was about eleven, I had to carry

the turkey down Bargate Street and around 'the shore' (Western Esplanade) to St. Michael's Square. The turkey weighed about sixteen pounds. Mr. Buckle took the bird and stuck a metal triangle in it. The triangle had a number on it. He then gave me a round disc with the same number on and told me when to return. Of course, he had dozens of other customers on Christmas day. I got back to Buckle's early to get to the front of the queue. I had to watch patiently as the various dishes were brought out of the oven and placed on the counter. There were all types of roasts – from large turkeys, to small bits of meat and it was not unknown for some crafty individual to switch triangles from a small joint to a large one, or even to a turkey. When the real owner came for his dinner he would be most upset. The baker's wife would often be called to keep her eye on the remaining dinners. That is why I made sure I was first in the queue.

I had a white cloth to cover the turkey and one to protect my hands from the hot roasting dish. I then had to struggle back to Bargate Street with the hot and heavy bird sitting in a dish of fat. By the time I got back to my uncle's house, every muscle ached. All this for sixpence – just two-and-a-half new pence!

Christmas was a dangerous time for people who had Christmas trees. There were no electric tree lights then, only candles to light it up. These were attached to the tree using little holders, which clipped onto the branches. The candleholders were made of tin and worked on the same principle as a pair of pliers, except that they had a strong spring to close the jaws on the branch. You had to be careful, because the ends of the jaws were serrated with teeth like a saw and could easily draw blood if you caught your finger. A lot of Christmas decorations were made of coloured paper so, as you can imagine, if a door was slammed, the rush of

This is my sister Louisa with her two pence doll.

air could either blow the candles out or could blow flames onto the decorations. Christmas could be more dangerous than the 5th of November, especially for girls with long hair and flowing dresses. Christmas tree accidents were quite frequent and sometimes fatal.

In the run up to Christmas, most children went carol singing. If it was cold, they carried 'winter warmers'. These were usually made from empty milk tins. The bottom was perforated with a nail; the tin was then stuffed with old cloth or cotton waste and a piece of wire was wrapped tightly around the tin with a cord attached to the end of it. The waste was then lit, the tin was whirled around your head with the string and the air was forced through the holes in the bottom of the tin causing a draught, which kept the rag burning. After a while, the tin got hot and you warmed your hands around your winter warmer. This little gadget lasted quite a long time and was great fun. There would always be someone who did not tie the wire tight enough round their tin and, as they twirled the tin round their head, it became loose and shot through the air like a bullet. A tin could weight about three-quarters of a pound and if it hit anyone, could be lethal. It could also smash through a window and cause a house fire.

The only place children could play was on the streets and everyone accepted this. Not many children had toys. We had to make our own amusements. The spinning top was a favourite game at that time of year, mainly because running after your top kept you warm!

Spinning a top sounds like a quiet game, but not with the tops *we* used. Our tops were called 'window breakers'. They were made of wood, were roughly the size and shape of a mushroom and cost a halfpenny. The ends of the 'stalks' were pointed and each had a metal stud inserted. The tops were about two and a half inches long and looked harmless, but in the hands of experts (that was us) they were lethal! Tops were spun from a standing position. You held the top between thumb and forefinger and would spin in by flicking your fingers and releasing it so that the top landed on the ground still spinning. You then struck it with a whip and the top would fly through the air for anywhere up to sixty feet. If it landed on hard ground, it would continue to spin and, when you reached it, you could strike it again. If a top went off-course and hit a window or a person, everyone promptly disappeared!

Southampton had a custom that died at the end of the thirties. On New Year's Eve we all gathered on the Asphalt, as it was called. The Asphalt was the part of Below Bar (Bar being short for Bargate) that extended from Holy Rood Church to the top of East Street. From about nine o'clock, young people gathered in this area, within the bounds of the corner of East Street, not into or over it. At the other end, the crowd did not cross into or over Bernard Street. Traffic stopped running at ten-thirty, by which time the road was virtually packed.

On New Year's Eve I was often at the Asphalt with my cousins, busy selling confetti, streamers and squirters (lead tubes, about twice the size of a tube of toothpaste, which were filled with water). To use the squirter, you unscrewed the top, squeezed the tube and a jet of water shot out. They were very popular with the men, who squirted the young ladies in all sorts of funny places.

As the time got close to twelve o'clock you could hardly move and everyone was in a party mood. Some wore party hats and funny fake noses; most had downed a couple of drinks, but there was never any trouble, just singing and dancing. We did a roaring trade with our streamers, confetti and squirters. Girls giggled and squealed as boys put confetti down the fronts of their dresses and used their squirters to good effect. Balloons popped, girls screamed and people laughed and sang. Everyone was happy.

When the magic hour arrived, the little men came out on the belfry of Holy Rood church and began to strike midnight. Everyone sang 'Auld Lang Syne' and kissed and wished each other a Happy New Year. The church bells rang throughout the town and all the ships in the port sounded their sirens. By a quarter past midnight the road was clear – everyone just disappeared.

8

THE STREETS OF SOUTHAMPTON

In the twenties and thirties, East Street was the centre of the town. At the top of East Street was All Saints Church, which was bombed in World War Two. This was my church, as I was christened there. It was a lovely building. The front, which faced onto the High Street, had large pillars either side of very imposing large doors. On the street outside the church was a stand for horse cabs. The horses were often fed from nosebags while their drivers sat patiently waiting for customers. In the latter part of the thirties, these cabs were replaced by taxis and the era of the horse cab came to an end.

Going down East Street, next to the church, was a pub called The Newcastle, and then came a tailor, then Carter's dry cleaners. The next shop was a small bazaar. We called it 'The Penny Bazaar' because on the step into the shop was an enlarged penny, about a yard in diameter. The Bazaar sold a cheap range of clothing and ornaments – all the sorts of things you would expect to see in a bazaar. If your change contained a farthing (a quarter of an old penny), the shop assistants always said they were out of farthings and would give you a packet of pins instead. The owners of The Bazaar came from the Midlands. Their names were Marks and

Spencer. Mr. Marks often visited the shop but no one ever saw his partner, Mr. Spencer.

Adjoining Marks' was another pub, The Brewery Bar, next to which was a large drapery shop called McIlroys, where, after a purchase, your money and your bill were put into a cup, which clipped onto a wire. The assistant would pull down on something similar to a toilet chain, there would be a click and the cup would shoot off to the cash office. You then had to wait for the cup to return with your receipt and change. Chairs were provided at the end of each counter for customers to sit and wait for their change.

Next to McIlroys was the turning for York Buildings. This now leads up to the Bargate Centre. On the opposite corner was a cycle maker named F.A. Hendy and Co. Ltd. When cars became more common, Hendy's became a garage. Hendy's expanded and moved twice. At the time of writing, they are at East Park Terrace. They have come a long way since I first knew of them.

When Hendy's moved, their premises in East Street (following extensive renovations) opened as the new and modern Marks and Spencer's. What a leap forward!

A few doors down the street was a beer retailer or beer shop. It was so called because it was not licensed for spirits or tobacco. The floors of beer shops were always sprinkled with large amounts of sawdust to soak up spillage, spittle from tobacco chewers and sometimes, blood. Fights were quite frequent and always bloody in those days.

Coopers Brewery was opposite York Buildings School. A little further down was (Mrs) Carlo, Fruiterer. Mrs Carlo was one of the first Italians to settle in Southampton. Another couple of shops, and you came to The Strand (which is approximately where Queens Way is now). This was another busy street, with a variety of shops on either side. One of these shops was Misslebrook and Weston, wholesale grocers. They had a shop on one side of The Strand and a large warehouse at the top end, facing the parks. Another shop of interest was Hollis Josiah – Jeweller and Pawnbroker.

There were more shops along East Street. One of these was Gough's the Butcher. I mention this shop because one section sold kosher meat only. The rabbi of the day used to stamp all meat and poultry that was fit for Jewish consumption. I remember the rabbi once telling us how to make an old hen taste tender. He said that he used to buy his hens live and, the night before he killed them, he would pour vinegar down their throats. Vinegar is a painkiller and it caused the hens' muscles to relax. The birds themselves were therefore relaxed when they were killed and their meat was always tender.

Next to Goughs stood another Misslebrook and Weston, which was next to a church called New Central Hall, set back about twenty feet. There were semi-circular steps leading up to the church door. New Central Hall was bombed during World War Two, then rebuilt. Next to this was Edwin Jones. There is a so-called mystery as to whether there was a walkway over East Street to Edwin Jones. The answer is yes with a capital 'Y'. As a boy I walked along this walkway many times to their warehouse on the opposite side of the street.

Why did they build a walkway over the street? Well, Edwin Jones needed to expand and needed more storerooms. At the end of their shop was a cut to the parks named Queens Buildings. On one side of the cut was Edwin Jones and on the opposite side was a row of cottages. The width of the cut was, at most, eight or nine feet, and the height of Edwin Jones' building cut off daylight to the cottages. The tenants eventually moved out and Edwin Jones bought the property for storage space. Before long, they wanted more.

Opposite Edwin Jones in East Street, next to Nelsons the pram shop and the post office, stood a large warehouse. The trouble was, the only entrance to the warehouse was from Orchard Lane. The entrance had large doors to allow lorries and carts to enter, but there was a problem – how to get goods to the shops? They could either take them across East Street and through the shop, or find another way. The only other way was to build a walkway from the warehouse to the shop. This was a simple job. A couple of girders were put in place to connect one side of the street to the other. A floor was laid between the girders and a galvanised cover was put over the top and windows were cut out of each side. Problem solved!

Edwin Jones' employees carried the goods from the warehouse to the shop in large wicker baskets or, in the case of long objects like carpets, lino or furniture, on flat trolleys, which had removable metal pins in each corner. The bridge was erected in the mid-twenties and was demolished when the front of the warehouse was converted into an extension of the shop. Unfortunately, all these interesting buildings were destroyed during the blitz.

I was in the Middle East when Edwin Jones was bombed. Lord Haw-Haw (William Joyce) informed us of the fact on the radio. Edwin Jones was a deliberate target because the shop had displayed a ME109 German fighter plane that had been shot down. The fighter was displayed to help collections for the Spitfire Fund. I have often wondered who told the Germans.

Edwin Jones had yet another shop further down East Street that was called a 'Boot Dealer'. A short distance from there was a cut called Houndwell Gardens and just below that, was Millers Cut, which was the scene of a very nasty murder during World War Two. A badly mutilated woman's body was found there and I don't think the murderer was ever caught. Ganges shoe shop was the last shop on that side of the road.

The first place of interest on the opposite side of East Street was a beer shop kept by Bill Tupper. Next to that was Kings Street, on the corner of which stood a fruit truck. The owner of the truck was quite a character. He was known as 'Cockney Green' and he used to attract customers with his witty remarks and often saucy placards. I remember one he wrote, which said, 'Come and have a pea my loves, come and have a pea.' This attracted a lot of attention, and 'Cockney' sold his peas!

Next, was the Standard Cinema, known to all and sundry as 'The Bug Hutch'. The front seats were benches; but the back had proper seats. As in all cinemas of the twenties, a piano was used for sound effects. Talking pictures, or 'talkies', were to come later. The pianist played appropriate music during different parts of the film. For example, during a love scene they would play a love song. If it was a cowboy film (a Western) and the baddies were chasing a stagecoach, the piano playing became frenzied and the audience became involved. If it was a war film, the pianist would sometimes have a drum, which was used to simulate canon fire. The piano would be played in a frenzy, and again the audience became involved by cheering when the enemy was being killed and making sympathetic noises when it was our side affected. I think the cinema was more fun during the era of silent films.

A little further up East Street was a shop known by seamen all over the world. It was called Georgie Beedle's. He sold all the uniforms and other working clothes for seamen. A boy just starting off to sea, maybe as a bell boy or deck boy, would sign on to his ship, then get a 'sub' (a loan to be deducted from his pay). He would then be directed to Georgie Beadle's, who stocked all the gear a seaman needed. A deposit was paid and they were fitted out. If lads grew out of their uniforms, Georgie would either part-exchange them or buy them back, providing they were in good condition.

Still further up was Orchard Lane. This was also a well-known road, with its lodging houses and Smith's the Coal Merchants. On buying coal from Smith, he would loan you a pair of iron trucks to wheel it home. The trucks were always returned. Smith also had a pair of hand trucks with a flat top. The police often borrowed these to transport drunks to the Bargate police station. The only official transport the police had were a couple of bicycles and a horse called Warrior, who was ridden by PC Strong. Warrior was an ex-army horse, and had been wounded in World War One. He is now buried at the Sports Centre.

Hepworths rag and bone merchant was also based in Orchard Lane. They bought rags at different prices, e.g. they paid less for mixed rags, more for sorted rags like whites or woollens. They also bought jam jars, bottles, bones, rabbit skins, old iron and all other metals.

My father owned a fruit truck on the corner of Orchard Lane, opposite Edwin Jones' warehouse, which took up a large part of East Street. Then there was The Anchor pub and, further up the street, was Nelson's pram shop and the post office. Further along, was Woolworth's; next to which was what I should think was the best-known pub in the maritime world, The Horse and Groom. The landlord then was Harry Batten. His wife became landlady when he died. She was a large woman, but very regal. She was the boss and she could quell trouble with a word and a look. Seamen from all over the world used The Horse and Groom. Prostitutes frequented the bar, but dared not be too obvious. There was also a huge stuffed bear in one corner. If you met seamen anywhere in the world and said you came from Southampton, they would invariably ask if you knew The Horse and Groom.

One side of The Horse and Groom was in 'The Ditches.' On the other side, a cut ran alongside the pub to a blacksmith's. I used to take my father's horse there to be shod or, when it was icy, to be clumped, which meant having bigheaded nails put in the horse's shoes to prevent it slipping.

'The Ditches' real name was Canal Walk. On the right-hand side a shop called Stanley and Co., Surgical Appliances still stands today. Another shop was Matchams, which sold fishing gear and all types of rope. In fact, everything pertaining to sailing boats. The stevedores also went to Matchams to buy their cargo hooks. Another shop I remember was Isaac, the newsagent. The owner was a widow with a large family who all went to York Building School. She kept cats that used to lie on the newspapers in the shop window. You could always smell them.

Farther up was Tommy White's restaurant, which catered to dockworkers. Tommy was an ex-professional boxer and was a friend of Joe Beckett, the British Heavyweight Champion, whose career came to an end when he was knocked out twice by the Frenchman, Le Carpenter, who became world champion.

Also in 'The Ditches' was the Council Girls Cookery Kitchen, the place poor children went for free meals. Along the top right-hand side of 'The Ditches' was a line of small shops built against the old town wall. These shops were just three or four feet deep and displayed their wares on shutters which, when lowered, turned into counters. They sold a variety of clothes, towels, curtains and such. These shops were kept by Jewish people and were the only shops open on a Sunday. For eleven pence and three farthings I could buy a pullover there and go to Sunday School looking tidy. 'The Ditches' also had its own pub, The Lord Roberts.

Going back into East Street, up to the back of The Walls, was a beer shop and a fruit truck, owned by a Mr. Ballard. The Back of The Walls had a brewery and a customs warehouse for wines and spirits.

The land on which the East Street multi-storey car park now stands was once a part of All Saints Cemetery, which at one time extended up to the High Street. The locals always said that no shop would prosper on that side of the street because it was sacred ground. Strangely, no shops seemed to last long there and, even now, people walk on the opposite side of the road.

Further up East Street was a cinema called The Picture Palace. A colourful character called Treswell once owned it. At one time, he aspired to become a town councillor and, to help his political campaign, he recruited about twenty boys and girls to march around his ward waving banners, which read, 'Vote for Treswell'. They also sang a song, which went like this, "Vote, vote, vote, for Mr.Treswell, who's that knocking at the door? If it's Morley and his wife, we will stab them with a knife, and we won't vote for Morley any more!" Sometimes Treswell would ride in an open tourer behind the chanting children, and would stand up and wave the Stetson-type hat he wore.

Just before the evening performance at The Picture Palace, Treswell's gang of youngsters marched down the centre isle waving banners and chanting the election song.

- *My Southampton* -

They were then seated on the front seats, which were long wooden benches, when an attendant marched down the isle with a basket of apples and gave the children an apple each. Finally, the candidate appeared to receive applause from the audience. He did not win the election, but the children enjoyed their part in it. There was no television and not many wireless sets in those days, so candidates for election had to canvas with their supporters around the streets to try to gain votes.

Another common and sad sight often seen in the twenties was that of ex-servicemen from the Great War (or World War One as it is now called), begging. Some wore placards around their necks, and sold matches. Others formed musical bands and walked the streets in single file playing any old instrument they had. Those who had no instruments collected money from the public using tins or their caps. They had to keep moving to avoid being arrested for obstruction. These were once proud men who had fought for a country that declared itself "Fit for heroes to live in".

There were also a lot of disabled people on the streets. Some of them had lost limbs, others were horribly disfigured. I will always remember one in particular. He had no legs and used to get around on a board with four metal wheels attached. He used his hands to propel the trolley along. The wheels were only three or four inches in diameter and to watch him manoeuver between pedestrians was a sight worth seeing. Never once did I see him hit anyone and he was one of the happiest people I have ever met. He crossed roads with ease and pavements were no obstacle to him – he would just put his arms straight down, let the trolley run, lower his trunk to the ground and whip the trolley onto the pavement. He would then straighten his arms, swing his body forward onto the pavement and then, in the same way, onto his trolley and away he would go. He was more agile than some people with two legs. I often wonder what happened to him.

One event I remember was when I was about 11 years old, no more. It must have been during the school holidays or on a Saturday morning and I was in East Street. Coming down the Ditches (Lower Canal Walk), were three men surrounded by a crowd of boys and girls all laughing and cheering. The middle one of the men wore only a vest and trousers. Hanging from his belt was a set of boxing gloves. His two mates were patting him on the back. as they walked up East Street and into a pub. I joined the crowd and waited outside the pub.

There was a lot of cheering and swearing coming from the pub and, after a short wait, the door opened and the three men reappeared. Two were supporting the one in the vest who now appeared to be covered in blood and was minus his boxing gloves. A crowd of men followed them out, all laughing and jeering. The three men staggered down East Street and through the Ditches. Apparently, they had come off an American ship, the *Leviathian*. The one in the vest had thrown down a challenge that he could beat any 'Limey B......d' in Southampton. In the pub, he met a ship's fireman who could not box but he could certainly fight! The boxing gloves probably ended up in Hollis, the pawnbrokers. I am very doubtful that the fighters stuck to Lord Queensbury's rules.

Seamen in those days worked hard and fought hard because life at sea was no fun for the men 'down below'. The stoke hold, where most of them worked, consisted of huge coalbunkers running along the ship's sides and the fires that heated the boilers.

The ships' firemen each had a bank of fires to stoke.

Each fireman had a 'trimmer' who had to supply him with coal. The temperature was incredibly high. The poor trimmer had to go to the bunker, load his iron barrow with coal, and run back and dump it by the side of the furnace door for the fireman to feed the fire. He had several boilers to supply and as the days went by he had farther to run as the bunkers emptied. If the trimmer slowed down, he took a lot of abuse from his fireman - both verbal and physical. The trimmers accepted this because they knew they would soon be firemen themselves and could treat their own trimmers in the same way!

The air below decks was filled with coal dust. People were forbidden to smoke, as one spark in a bunker could ignite the airborne coal dust and cause a flash fire which would burn everyone in the stoke hold. The stoke hold had forced pressure, so when the fire doors opened, air rushed in, allowing no sparks to get out. On very rare occasions a fire would blow back and heaven help the firemen if it did. You can see why these men were hard. Violence was a part of life.

On Saturday nights, every pub was full. I can remember there being eight pubs in East Street, although some were classified as beer shops because they did not have licenses to sell wine and spirits.

A lot of seamen used the East Street pubs, especially the 'down below' crowd - the stokers, trimmers, greasers and firemen. As previously mentioned, men could not smoke while on watch. In addition to the danger of sparks from cigarettes or pipes, a cigarette would have been a soggy mess in no time in the stoke hold because men would run with sweat for the whole of their watch. Instead of smoking, some men used snuff, while others chewed tobacco. I know some men who, when ashore, did all three, so you can see

Bellboys, the maiden voyage of the Queen Mary. *My younger brother Walter is on the right front row.*

why most pubs had sawdust on the floor. Some men were not at all particular and would spit a stream of tobacco juice onto the floor of the pub and not into the spittoons or the floor troughs that ran around the edge of the bar.

There were fruit trucks on nearly every street corner. At night, each one was lit by a paraffin lamp. These worked on the same principle as a primus stove – with a pump to keep the pressure in the tank. A brass or copper pipe, about twenty inches long, ran from the tank and was bent into a u-shape. The burner was screwed to the end of the pipe and was similar to the type found on a gas stove. Another screw was inserted where the pipe was connected to the tank. To light the lamp you first pumped air into the tank, then lit a piece of newspaper and inserted the burner into the flames. You had to wait for the burner to get hot before turning the screw. The paraffin vaporised when it got to the hot burner, producing flames around the edge and making a really effective light. The lamps were always hung on poles attached to the stalls and were also useful for keeping hands warm on cold nights.

Paraffin was not as clean as it is today and dirt would sometimes clog the holes, extinguishing lamps, spraying hot oil everywhere and emitting oily black smoke. On these occasions, you had to act quickly and turn off the oil supply to the burner. You would then prick the holes in the burners with fine wire to clear the obstructions, after which the lamps could be re-lit. If the stalls got sprayed with oil, the consequences could be very expensive for the stallholders, or 'costers', as they were then called.

The costers had their own union branch, which was part of the Transport and General Workers Union. The chairman was Bill Dart who had a stall on Kingsland Square. All the barrow boys and stallholders were members.

- The Streets of Southampton -

Southampton's Kingsland market was a lot different in those days. It was an open market and the stallholders were all locals. An old Jewish gentleman called Mr. Harris ran one stall. He dealt mostly in second-hand clothes and you would see his customers trying on jackets and other items, often arguing and haggling over the price, but invariably leaving satisfied. I remember a home-made sweet stall and there was Jacko Davis, who used to be called The Bacon King. He was a real character who sold bacon cheaper than anyone else and had quite a way with his lady customers, who seemed to like his somewhat bawdy jokes.

Tom Hampton and Bill Dart ran vegetable stalls. Bill had a character all his own. He was quite a size and always joked and laughed with his customers. Many of the old market traders remained in Kingsland Square for many years and some of their grandchildren hold the same stalls today.

In the thirties, for one or two old pence, you could buy enough 'pot herbs' to make a good stew – if a pennyworth of bones was added. Pot herbs consisted of carrots, onions, swede, and parsnips. A nutritious meal for the whole family could be provided for about fourpence.

There used to be two large bakers shops in Above Bar. Price's Bakery was on one side of the road and Lowman's Bakery was opposite. Many a time after school, armed with a large shopping bag and two old pence (just over one present-day penny), I would go first to Price's, which was a large, high-class shop and ask for tuppence worth of stale cakes. If I was lucky, one of the assistants would empty tray after tray of unsold cakes in to my bag. There would be vanilla slices, iced cakes, buns, and every type of cake that was left at the end of the day. All this for two pence! Today, I often see cakes and bread on sale in supermarkets at reduced prices. However, the cheapest of those is five

Above: My cousins Violet and Henry against the old walls. Vi was the Pearly Queen and the fruit truck was a common sight on the streets of the town. The round baskets were cherry baskets. Henry drove one of the first T Fords in Southampton. Vi is the only survivor of her

family of fifteen brothers and sisters. Today she can be seen selling her flowers in Queens Way opposite Debenhams.

Left: My cousin Molly taken against the old walls, note the car headlight. She was in Southampton carnival as a flower girl in late twenties.

times more than I paid for a whole bag of Price's cakes! If Price's had already got rid of their stale cakes, I would go across to Lowman's. Needless to say, I was not the only one waiting for stale cakes. It was first come, first served, but I was not often disappointed. A bag of cakes lasted a few days and what our family didn't eat we gave to others. Everyone was poor but they shared. That was a way of life.

It was in the late twenties or early thirties that the Echo newspaper sellers of Southampton went on strike. A man called Dave Parish led them. The reason for the strike was the fact 'paperboys' did not get a refund on unsold papers. This meant a substantial loss, because selling papers was their sole source of income. Luckily the strike was short. The *Echo* quickly reached a settlement with the paperboys, who were the main means of conveying news in those days – television was non-existent and wireless was expensive.

Paperboys started early in the day with the morning papers. Some had newspaper rounds, some had stands and others sold their papers at factory gates and dock gates. Each day's *Echo* started with a first-edition morning paper, then an afternoon paper, the *Evening Echo*, a final edition and a late night final edition. Quite a few editions per day! On Saturday, they published the *Football Echo*. The football pools started in this era and people bought the *Football Echo* to check and find out if they had won a fortune or not. The paper also included horse racing results and 'the dogs' – greyhound racing results.

Gambling was a way of life for the working classes. If it wasn't football, horses or dogs, it was cards, dominoes, or shove-halfpenny. Shove-halfpenny was a skilful game played on a slate board, which had lines marked across that were just wide enough for a halfpenny to fit into. The game (played today with different coins) was between two players and the idea was to get the most halfpennies between the lines. To watch good players was an education. Each player placed a halfpenny coin at the bottom edge of the board and then struck it with the heel of the hand to try and get it between the lines. If I remember correctly, we used five coins, all highly polished on one side. The board was dusted with French chalk so, if you tapped a coin wrongly, it skidded off the board. Good players used to be able to nudge coins between lines by using other coins to tap them. Each set of lines had to have three coins in it. You had to be skilful to win. It was harder than playing computer games. Once you have mastered a computer game, it becomes easier to play. With shove-halfpenny, no two games are ever the same. The game was often played for a pint of beer.

The paperboys used to gamble among themselves while waiting for their papers to come off the press. They could be found outside the slaughterhouse, next to the *Echo* Office in Spa Road. They would play cards or be 'Up in the line', which was a line drawn or scratched on the pavement. The players lined up and pitched pennies to see who could get closest to the line. The winner took all. Another game was pitch and toss, where a line of coins would be placed on the hand and flicked into the air. The idea was to guess if the coins would land heads or tails up. An odd number of coins were used. The caller (who had won the right to call by tossing a coin) would place the coins on his hand either heads up or tails up. He then tossed the coins in the air at the same time shouting 'heads' or 'tails'. After landing, the coins were eagerly inspected. If the tosser had called 'heads' and the total number of coins with heads up was higher than those with tails up, he would win. Non-players would often make side bets.

Two things interrupted these games. One was a police raid, which was not usually successful because there was always a small boy on lookout or 'skite' as it was called. He would give a distinctive warning whistle. When heard, everyone scattered – usually running down into Spa Gardens to hide until the police gave up the search.

The other thing that sometimes upset a game was market day. Southampton cattle market was held on a Wednesday. The market was located next to the railway bridge in Bridge Road (now a housing complex). Sheep, cattle, pigs, chickens; almost anything was sold there – from old bikes to horses. The cattle were brought to market in various types of vehicles – from old horse-drawn wagons which had nets over the animals to prevent them jumping out, to old army lorries that had been converted for transporting animals. Some cattle were driven on foot and were transported across the river Itchen via the floating bridges. The floating bridges would be sectioned off so that the animals could be penned for the crossing. Passengers travelled on the outer sides of the bridges, safe from the animals. Can you imagine cattle, sheep, pigs and goats being driven through Woolston, sometimes with dogs helping the drovers, and the odd sheep or cow trying to escape from the main herd or flock? The local boys tried to be helpful, but were far from it. On market day, shopkeepers closed their doors and stood outside to protect any wares they had on display.

The animals left their calling cards (droppings!) in the road, on pavements and, if you were unlucky, in people's doorways. They also left the accompanying smells! Another complication was the increasing use of cars and lorries that helped spray the mess on all and sundry.

Once driven to the market and sold, many cattle went for slaughter. These had to be driven up Oxford Street, into the High Street near Holy Rood church and up and through the Bargate. This sometimes caused problems because all three arches were always in use; the main one was for traffic, the other two for pedestrians. The cattle had to be driven through the center arch, but some did not wish to go that way. The sheep were the worst offenders, as sometimes they would try and make for one or both of the smaller arches. As there was usually only one drover, this was often a problem. If a sheep managed to get through the left arch they could turn down Bargate Street. If they went through the right arch, they could either turn right into a court next to Kim's Cozy Corner pub (where they could easily be caught) or they could run seventy-five yards, turn right and gallop down Hanover Buildings to the parks. The drovers' job was made harder by pedestrians, most of whom were women, screaming and waving handbags and shopping bags in the air. Traffic was often held up on market day. The policemen, whose job it was to control the traffic going through the Bargate arches would try to maintain order, while sheep, bewildered by it all, would run in all directions.

Beef cattle were easier to drive, but when a problem arose it could be very dangerous. I remember a bull getting as far as the slaughterhouse where it suddenly gave a great bellow (it must have smelled blood). It swung round, knocking the drover for six and belted down Spa Road into Above Bar. In no time there was pandemonium. Shoppers screamed and tried to get out of the way. Traffic stopped; people fell off bikes and the bull headed towards the Bargate. Panic was the order of the day. Luckily, the bull ran down Hanover Buildings and into the parks, where it was eventually cornered and shot. Apart from some people getting a few bruises and a couple of ladies fainting, no one was seriously hurt. As a boy, it made my day!

9

BOMBS IN BARGATE STREET

In about 1928, we moved from Tower Place. The children in our family had expanded to five boys and one girl and my grandmother also lived with us. The house we moved to seemed like heaven. It had a gas supply and electric lights! It was quite a large house, but, as in Tower Place, the back wall was part of the old Town Walls. So again, there were no windows at the rear, but because it was large and double-fronted, every room had a window.

We had an underground kitchen which had a ground-level window about one foot tall by two feet long. Walking down to the kitchen seemed like going back hundreds of years in time. The spiral steps that led down were well-worn stone. The walls were built of the same stones as the old parts of the town and there was a dark alcove that went back about six feet. The stone floor was cold and uneven. If it was not for the old sink, which was also stone and had a cold water tap, the gas cooker and the big copper boiler, the kitchen could have been exactly as when it was built hundreds of years before.

When we moved into the house, the cellar was the first place I explored. There was an electric light in the ceiling, but it had only a low-voltage bulb and the light did not penetrate into the corners or alcoves. In one of the alcoves, I found a shelf with a rather large, heavy box. I carried it

This is my mother with Bill left, Maureen and Len. Furs were fashionable then.

into the light to examine the contents. To my amazement, it was filled with different types of grenades – British Mills bombs, German stick bombs and various other types, plus a couple of pineapples – the first aerial bombs. Those were round and segregated like a Mills bomb and weighed four or five pounds. Pilots used to keep them in the cockpits of their planes and drop them by hand on their targets. A pretty hit-and-miss affair!

When my father saw my treasure, he made me take the box to the police station, which was about 50 yards up the road. When the desk sergeant saw what was in the box, he almost had a blue vinegar fit! He said there were enough explosives there to blow up the street and then told me they would be dumped in the river.

Soon after we moved in, I went into my grandmother's room to find her standing on a chair, wrapping newspaper round the electric bulb holder. I asked her what she was doing and her reply was that she did not want anything to do with these new-fangled things and the paper was to stop anything coming out of the holder. She insisted on using her trusted candlestick until the day she died.

The car park located next to Arundel Towers was once my uncle's yard. It used to be approximately 80 yards long by 40 feet wide. You entered the yard through two, eight feet high doors at the bottom of Tower Place. Inside the yard was a large, two-storey shed in which he stored his old Model-T Ford truck, plus a variety of fruits and flowers. He and his family had a thriving business working various Hampshire markets with fruit stalls. He was also one of the biggest watercress growers in the south. Two of his daughters (my cousins) sold flowers from the pavement next to the parks in Above Bar. They usually stood just below the clock tower, which was in the middle of New Road, where it joined Above Bar.

The clock was later moved to Bitterne Triangle. Besides housing a clock, the clock tower had a built-in water trough for horses and a waterspout for people, next to which was an iron cup attached to a chain. The water was always stone cold. As a lad, I had quite a few drinks from that cup - as did hundreds of others, all strangers - but I never heard of anyone getting ill from it.

Arundel Tower was built against the old walls and built against the tower was a builder's workshop. As a lad, I often played in my uncle's yard with my brothers, sister and cousins. In one part of the yard was a pile of rubble, and sticking out of the rubble I remember two stone monuments resembling deer. They were on stone bases and both were damaged. We never took much notice of them because they were just rubbish as far as we were concerned. Years later

My cousin Nell and me in 1934. I was on weekend leave, note the army haircut. Arundel Tower is behind with shed built on to it.

when people started looking for the stone deer that were missing from Stag Gates, in The Avenue, I remembered the monuments that were dumped in my uncle's yard.

The strange thing was that the builder's workshop, another large shed on the opposite side of Bargate Street and several builders' ladders were never used. I can't even remember seeing any workmen there either. I wonder who the builder was? Was he the contractor who demolished Stag Gates?

In those days (now more than 80 years ago) people never dreamed of saving things for posterity. Workmen would not have used scaffolding to dismantle the pillars on which the Stag Gates deer were placed. They probably just removed bricks from the bases and, with the aid of ropes and, possibly, a horse, pulled the pillars down. The rubble would then have been carted away, the best bricks saved and the rubble transported to my uncle's yard – rubble which included two damaged deer that had no further use.

The gates had been demolished in the name of progress – overhead cables had to be installed for the new tramcars, which were driven by electricity.

In about 1932, we moved house again; this time to Grove Street. There, we had a shop with living accommodation, stables, a garage and ample room for fruit trucks and storage. The stable was a Godsend because it meant our horse was at hand for feeding and cleaning. My father used our horse only one day a week – on Sundays. He had a sales round where, from his two-wheeled flat cart, he sold fruit, watercress and winkles. His round was the Woolston area. His white horse, named Daisy, was a New Forest pony. All of his customers made a fuss of Daisy and always gave her tit-bits. There are people who still remember dad and his white pony. They also remember their Sunday tea of bread, butter, winkles and watercress. That was also our tea.

Dad used to get his winkles from Warsash, where he bought them from the winkle pickers. The winkle pickers went out at low tide and collected winkles from the mud. My father bought a half-hundredweight every Saturday night on his way home from Fareham, where he had a stall in the Royal Oak yard. He used to get home at about 10 o'clock at night and the winkles had to be washed and cooked. The copper would be ready and, once washed, the winkles would be put in the copper with a block of salt and boiled ready for the Woolston round the next day.

The bait diggers of this period did not have thigh boots (they couldn't afford them) but they still used to go out on the mud flats to dig bait because every one of them had a pair of 'mud pats'. These were two squares of wood, about an inch or so thick by about a foot square. The bait diggers

This picture was taken on a Sunday morning and shows my father's cart loaded with fruit, flowers, winkles and watercress ready to go on his round to Woolston. Winkles and watercress was Sunday tea.

Daisy, my father's pony. He bought her at the forest pony sales and walked back to Southampton leading her. She was a great favourite of his customers.

made two holes in each piece of wood, then looped a piece of rope through and tied a large knot under the pats to stop the rope coming back through the holes. They then attached the pats to their boots by the rope. Thus equipped, they were able to walk on the mud without sinking. I am surprised that firemen have not adopted the idea for when they have to rescue people or animals from mud.

During this period, the Salvation Army was always in evidence. The Salvation Army band could be seen all over the town. The bottom of East Street was an especially popular place. When they preached, it was real 'fire and brimstone' preaching. One incident I always remember was when the band came up Grove Street playing their music. In one of the houses lived an older man, who had (for some unknown reason) been thrown out of the 'Sally Ann'. As the band passed his house, 'Old Charlie' fell in at the rear and started marching. The bandleader noticed him and started to remonstrate with him, saying he was no longer a 'soldier'. Charlie ignored him and carried on. The bandleader tried to push Charlie out of the parade. He would push, poor old Charlie would stagger, and then back he would come to continue marching. This carried on until the band marched out of Grove Street with onlookers laughing aloud. As they left Grove Street, Charlie returned, having proven his point. All the neighbours cheered and clapped as he swaggered down the middle of the road. I have often wondered what he had done to get thrown out. Charlie was one sinner who was not welcomed back to the fold.

Women never went into public bars in those days, apart from those in the Salvation Army, who were always welcome. On weekends, the women of the Sally Ann would walk around selling their paper, the *War Cry*. As East Street was full of pubs, they would go inside with a bundle of papers, calling, "War Cry". Invariably, if they were young, they would not be allowed to leave until they sang a hymn. They did not mind this because they knew if they sang they would sell copies of *War Cry*. They also enjoyed the banter as much as the men did.

10

LIFE AND DEATH ON THE RIVER; BUILDING THE NEW DOCK

The last major event of the nineteen-thirties in Southampton was the building of the New Dock. Britain, with the exception of Wales (where unemployment was the highest in the nation) was just pulling out of the Depression and the contractors for the New Dock turned to the Welsh for their labour force. The poor men they hired were paid slave wages, which they were forced to accept because they were starving. As they could not afford lodgings they had to live on-site and they made shelters out of anything they could find. All the money they earned was sent home to their starving families.

Ironically, the contractors wound up paying dearly. In fact, most of them went bankrupt. The problem was that, to build the dock, a lot of land had to be recovered from the sea. At Millbrook, the sailing club had to go to make way for development. The biggest problem was where to start the dock wall. Piles (which had to be driven into the mud) were lost because they could not find ground firm enough to sink them in. Before this problem was solved, many firms went bust. Everything was eventually solved and the quay wall was finally built.

The next job was to drain and fill the reclaimed land. To reach the working area, the men had to walk across hundreds of wooden ducks. In places, if a man fell off the ducks, he could drown in the soft mud. As the ground was reclaimed, the on-site workers had to move too, and they slept like animals in their rough shelters. Some of the younger unmarried workers went to the local pubs at weekends. There they would get drunk and have to make their way back to their shelters across the uneven wooden walkways. In some places a slip of the foot could mean certain death. Unfortunately, the inevitable did happen – a man would not turn up for work and, maybe, his cap would be found on the mud. In the pay office, there were sometimes unopened wage packets of workers who had disappeared in the mud.

As boys, we often went out on the mud flats to talk to the men and listen to them singing. They loved to sing, although they did not have much to sing about.

All the dustcarts, clinker lorries and carts from the gas works helped to fill in the reclaimed land and horse-drawn tankers cleared the drains. The filling in was a tedious operation as carts and lorries drove to the edge of the landfill and dumped their loads over the edge. There were always fifteen to twenty men waiting for the rubbish to be dumped. They started by sifting the ash and clinker, looking for pieces of coal, or partly burned coal, which they put into sacks on homemade trucks and old prams. The sacks of 'coal' were sold for a few coppers. Another group of men sorted through the rubbish dumped from the dustcarts, looking for scrap metal, brass, copper, lead, scrap iron and anything else they could sell. There was yet another group of men who waited where the tanks that collected mud and sludge from the towns drains, dumped their loads.

These men waited until the surplus water had drained away, then, armed with pieces of hoop iron, they scraped the surface of the mud, looking for coins. If they were lucky, they found rings that had fallen down the drains. Some of these once-proud men had fought in the Great War and were now reduced to scavenging in mud and filth to earn a few extra coppers to keep their families from starving. Great Britain had an empire that covered nearly half the world and British men were reduced to this.

As the ground was reclaimed, large pylons were erected for the cables that would be needed to supply electrical power to the docks. One such pylon was erected opposite West Station (now Central Station). Six men were perched at the top of the pylon, working on its arms, when, without warning, the steel tower fell over, killing all six. The price of the New Dock was rising.

One of the many cargoes to come into the port was timber. Some of this was bulk timber; large lengths of wood, some about twenty or thirty feet long and twelve to sixteen inches square. The bulk timber was usually destined for the large timber companies on the banks of the River Itchen. The easiest way to get the wood to the timber yards was by water. The dockers lowered the lengths of timber over the ship's side into the water. This in itself was a dangerous operation, as other dockers either waited in the water in rowing boats, or climbed over the ship's side and balanced on the timbers in order to pull them together to make huge rafts. They started with two bulks of timber. The dockers had two coils of rope, two tins of large staples, two boat hooks and a tool with a hammerhead at one end and an axe head at the other. To make the raft, they stapled rope tightly from one log to the other, and then attached rope to each end. They made the raft wider by attaching more timber as it was lowered down the side of the ship. The dockers pushed the logs from the ship's side allowing more logs to be lowered into the water. Sadly, if the logs slipped, the dockers stood no chance.

Thus, huge rafts were made and were towed up the Itchen to be moored along the banks and shores of Chapel and Northam before being taken to local sawmills. When the tide went out, parts of the rafts were grounded, whilst the rest remained afloat. They could cover a large area, sometimes over one hundred yards by one hundred yards. This area would increase as new timber ships arrived in the port. You can imagine this sea of floating logs bobbing up and down on the water.

The local children were used to playing by the water. They also played on the rafts. They knew it was dangerous, but to growing children, danger is an added attraction. To run across the logs and feel them move under your feet was great fun. The danger lay in the fact that, with the movement of the river and the wash of passing boats, a rope would sometimes loosen, or staples would pull out, allowing logs to drift part. If a person stepped on an insecure log, it would separate from the rest and in you could go. If that happened where the water was deep, you stood no chance of survival as you would sink under the logs and not be able to surface. Any older resident of Northam or Chapel will remember children or adults who died in this manner. The last time I remember such a tragedy was when two children drowned. (I became a docker after the war and helped to construct timber rafts).

In the mid-twenties there was a major accident on the river, when one of the floating bridges sank. Each of the two floating bridges ran on two heavy cables, which went from a hard on the Southampton side to a hard on the

Woolston side of the river Itchen. A ship going down the river severed the cables of one of the bridges with its bow. The person operating the floating bridge either did not notice the ship, or thought it could reach the opposite shore in time. It was a bad error. As the bow of the ship cut through the cables, it spun the floating bridge out like a cork, causing it to float down the river and sink.

Fortunately, there were only a few people aboard and they were saved. Each floating bridge carried a rowing boat and, with the help of another boat from Thornycroft's, the passengers were evacuated. The only loss of life was a large shire horse belonging to Southern Railway. He drowned because he was attached to his cart. The bridge sank off Thornycroft's yard, but was soon recovered and put back in service. If this accident had happened a few hours earlier, the bridge would have been packed with workers and there would have been many deaths.

An old hulk, which I believe originally housed French prisoners of war, but had been converted to a hospital ship, was moored between Hythe and Southampton during the twenties. We always called it 'The Fever Ship' because it was used to house people with infectious diseases. I was told that my grandfather died from typhoid fever on this ship. In 1925, it was listed as an amenity of the town and remained in use until the Western Hospital was built.

If you search the mud flats of Woolston and Western Shore, between the sewage plant and the yacht club, you can still find clay pipes and other articles that came from the hospital ship. If you are lucky, you may find ornamental pipes with figures of men or animal heads on them. My sons found some of these in the sixties.

11

TRAMS AND TRAFFIC

I have written about life in Southampton, as I knew it, during the twenties and thirties, and will finish with the reason the roundabout was built around the Bargate – Southampton's well-known landmark. Many of you will know how the Bargate used to look from old photos, taken when it had adjoining buildings. On the Above Bar (north) side of the Bargate, was Kim's Cozy Corner, a very popular little pub. On the High Street (south) side were the Law Offices and Magistrates rooms. Inside the Bargate, the room on the upper level was a courtroom. As you went through the arches from Above Bar, there were solicitors' offices to the left and the Bargate Hotel to the right.

In the early twenties the main means of transport was the tram. Tramlines led to every part of the town and the trams were used extensively. For one old penny you could travel from the Bargate to The Common. There were two types of tram, one with an open top, the other covered like a present-day bus. The covered trams, with their square roofs, could not pass through the Bargate arches. They were later fitted with rounded tops so that people could travel in comfort in all weathers.

In the summer, it was fine to ride on the top deck of an open tram, but in winter or when it rained, it was very uncomfortable. Imagine a cold, wet morning when you would get on your tram to work only to find the lower deck full and the only available space being on the upper deck. You could not sit up there because the seats were wet. In all probability, you had no topcoat or Mac, so stood with others looking like penguins and feeling miserable and wet. If you smoked a cigarette it would become a soggy mess. Most of the passengers travelling to town were dockworkers who came from areas like Shirley, Portswood or Swaythling. It was a long ride and they had to work in their wet clothes all day. In those days, if you did not turn up for work (wet or not) you were sacked.

At 'knocking-off time' (the end of the day), trams lined up at the Floating Bridge, The Pier and other points. They would all be packed. Due to the railway-line mode of operation, trams could not be turned around. They had to be driven from one end of the line to the other. There were steps at each end of each tram leading to the upper deck. If a tram was packed with passengers, people would also stand on the stairs. A conductor collected passengers' fares.

There were two sets of tramlines, running in different directions, throughout the town, with the exception of the Bargate, where there was only room for one tram to pass through. All forms of traffic had to pass through the Bargate arches, as there was no way around it then.

To control the problem of right-of-way, a set of traffic lights was placed either end of the main arch. These were controlled by a policeman who was stationed by one of the lions on the Above Bar side. He had a junction box attached to the wall, which had a lever on the side. There were only two lights, which, if I remember correctly, said, 'Halt' and 'Pass'. A policeman was on duty whenever the trams ran. When it rained, the policeman wore a large, white rubber Mac, which was always hung on the wall when not in use.

Where the sets of tram lines converged to a single track there was a set of points which were controlled by the tram driver, with a bar that had a flattened end. As the tram came to the points, he would lean over and flick them with the bar.

There was very little motor traffic in the early twenties. There were few motorcars, but still a lot of horse traffic, plus the odd Foden steam wagon, which were large lorries driven by steam engines. These were trains that carried most of the goods that came in on the boats. Road traffic that needed to go north had to go under the Bargate.

Tollgates surrounded the town (Northam, top of the Avenue and Eling, to name but a few). There was only one clear way out of Southampton and that was north. On the east, west and south you had to cross water. From Above Bar, if you wanted to get to Western Esplanade you had to go down steep hills. Manchester Street was then so steep horses could not use it.

Halfway down Manchester Street was a saddler. One day, about six lads (I'm sorry to say I was one of them) went down Manchester Street and saw two wicker chairs, which were made for invalids, sitting outside the saddler's shop. These had cane frames and three wheels; two large ones at the back and a small one at the front. They were made so that the invalid sat in them as if in a chair and guided themselves with a long handle attached to the front wheel. At the back of the chair was a bar, which was used to push it. Now, seeing these chairs as two 'chariots', two of the lads got into them and two pushed. Our chariots soon started to go faster than the lads could run... so they let go! The chariots charged downhill with the drivers shouting their heads off whilst trying to steer straight. One ended up against the public baths, the other turned over about three times. No one was hurt, but the wheelchairs certainly needed repairs. We were lucky there was hardly any traffic, but this would soon alter as cars became more popular. Soon, horses began to disappear from the roads and people were able to travel long distances in shorter times. Some of the toll bridges disappeared and a new bridge had to be built at Bitterne Triangle to accommodate the increase in traffic. The last tollgate in the area is still operating. This is situated at Eling and is only free if you are attending a funeral.

Where once the policeman at the Bargate used only to deal with trams and maybe a horse cab or brewer's dray, traffic now started to build up on either side of the Bargate. Something had to be done, so it was decided that a road should be built around one side of the Bargate. Curry's had to be demolished, as did Kim's Cozy Corner and many other shops. It was not until after the war that the road on the other side was completed. The Bargate now stands impressively isolated, like an island.

I strongly believe that the Bargate should be a National Monument. No other building in the land has its history, which goes back centuries. British armies have marched through the Bargate on their way to and from wars. The Pilgrim Fathers, founders of America, must surely have passed through an arch of the Bargate, down West Gate Street to board the *Mayflower*.

In 1934, I joined my county regiment, the Hampshire Regiment, and in January 1st 1937 I sailed with them from Southampton on the vessel *Nevassa*. I returned at the end of 1943 to a Southampton that was barely recognizable after the bombing raids of World War Two, but, thank God, standing proud amongst all the destruction was the Bargate. The town was badly wounded but its heart was sound. The

- My Southampton -

Bargate still looks out over our city. What other changes
will she see?